IGCSE
Study Guide

for Business Studies

Karen Borrington and Peter Stimpson

HODDER
EDUCATION
AN HACHETTE UK COMPANY

Orders: please contact Bookpoint Ltd, 130 Milton Park, Abingdon, Oxon OX14 4SB.
Telephone: (44) 01235 827720. Fax: (44) 01235 400454. Lines are open from 9.00–5.00,
Monday to Saturday, with a 24-hour message answering service.
Visit our website at www.hoddereducation.co.uk

© Karen Borrington and Peter Stimpson
First published in 2005 by
Hodder Education, An Hachette UK Company
338 Euston Road
London NW1 3BH

Impression number   10 9 8 7 6 5
Year   2010 2009

Cover photo © Corbis/Stockmarket, Matthias Kulka
Typeset in 12/14pt Bembo by Pantek Arts Ltd, Maidstone, Kent
Printed and bound in Great Britain by CPI Antony Rowe

A catalogue record for this title is available from the British Library

ISBN: 978 0 719 57901 1

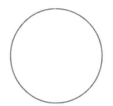

Contents

Introduction

How to use the study guide

This text has primarily been written to support students in their study of Business Studies to IGCSE. It has been designed to complement the *IGCSE Business Studies* textbook (Borrington and Stimpson). The units in this guide follow the chapters in the textbook.

Please be aware, however, that the order of the units in the textbook and this study guide and the order of the sections of the curriculum content are different. Teaching programmes do not have to follow the order of either the curriculum content in the syllabus or the textbook. Teachers may have used the scheme of work provided on CIE's website, so again the order of the units in this study guide will not be the same as the order of topics in the scheme of work, or the scheme of work provided on the CD-ROM which supports the textbook.

IGCSE Syllabus – Curriculum Content	IGCSE Study Guide Units
Business and the environment in which it operates:	
A – Business activity	Units 1, 2
B – The organisation	Units 1, 2
C – Changing business environment	Units 4, 5
D – Economic environment	Units 1, 2, 25
Business structure, organisation and control:	
A – Ownership and internal organisation	Units 3, 10, 11, 12
B – Financing business activity	Unit 9
Business activity to achieve objectives:	
A – Marketing	Units 16, 17, 18, 19, 20, 21, 22
B – Production (Operations management)	Units 6, 23, 24
C – Financial information and decision-making	Units 7, 8
People in business:	
A – Human needs and rewards	Unit 13
B – Manpower	Unit 14
Regulating and controlling business activity:	
A – Reasons for regulation	Units 4, 5
B – Influences on business activity	Units 4, 5, 15, 25

The IGCSE Business Studies examination has two question papers. Paper 1 contains short-answer questions and structured questions based on short pieces of information. The skills being tested are mainly knowledge with understanding and application, with fewer marks awarded for analysis and evaluation. The questions on this paper carry up to 8 marks, but most of the questions have 2, 3, 4, 5 or 6 marks allocated. You will see in the different units in the study guide there are these types of shorter-answer questions for you to practise.

Paper 2 has a business situation or problem with questions arising from the case study. The skills being tested on this paper are analysis and evaluation, but the questions will be asking for the answer to be applied to the business in the case study. The questions on this paper often carry 8, 10 or 12 marks. Again, there are questions in the different units in this book, which will help you to practise answering these types of questions.

Each unit in the study guide has the following five sections:

Section	What the section covers	How to use the section
Key objectives	Outlines the key objectives, which specify what you should understand or be able to do in the examination.	These lists can serve as a checklist of your progress in each topic.
Key definitions	Summarises the main terms or definitions you should know for the examination.	These are only summaries (in the form of a table or diagram) and for more detailed explanation you should add to these from your textbook or class notes.
Sample questions and answers	Gives examples of student answers, outline mark schemes and examiner's marks and comments.	Cover up the examiner's marks and comments and see what mark you would have given the answer before you look at the actual mark that was given. This will help you understand what is required for full marks.
Common misconceptions and errors	Gives some common mistakes made by students in exams.	
Try this	Has examination questions for you to answer.	Answer the questions. The answers section at the back of this revision guide will help you to check the marks your answer would have received.

This study guide contains the necessary support for the attainment of the highest grade. It can be used on its own or in combination as follows:

- to complement the IGCSE textbook and CD-ROM
- at the end of each topic, to provide reinforcement and assessment
- to prepare for the IGCSE examination.

If you want to get the maximum value from this book, it is strongly advised that you attempt to answer all the questions on paper and not in the book. Then you can repeat the exercises at intervals throughout the course.

We hope you find this book a useful resource in your study of IGCSE Business Studies and that it assists you in gaining a commendable grade.

What examiners are looking for

Most Business Studies examination papers are testing four different skills. These are:

- knowledge with understanding
- application
- analysis
- evaluation.

Knowledge with understanding. This is tested with the type of question that asks you to explain a particular term, for example, 'What is meant by market segment?' These are the type of questions where you will need to have revised the terms or definitions of the different topics. You need to be able to write down what they mean clearly and accurately if you are to gain maximum marks. With thorough revision of the definitions section and supporting notes it will be relatively easy to acquire most of the marks for these questions. Unfortunately, only about a quarter of the marks across the whole papers will be for knowledge with understanding.

The type of command words which are testing this area are: Describe…, State…, List…, Outline…, What is meant by…, Give…, Define…, Identify…, Name…

Application. This means the examiner is testing whether you can apply your answer to the business given in the examination, for example, 'What do you think the business in the case study could do to increase sales?' Your answer must not just be a general explanation of how a business could increase sales, but how this specific business could increase sales. If you don't try to think in terms of the business given, you will lose a quarter of the marks across the whole examination papers. So this is a very important skill.

When you look at the revision questions in this book, you will see that there are many mini case studies outlined before the questions themselves so that you can practise this skill of answering in the context of the particular business.

The type of command words which are testing this area are: Explain how this business…, Why might company x…, Give an example from the case study to…, Why might company z…, From the case study outline…

Analysis. The skill of analysis involves being able to select information from text, tables, graphs, diagrams or drawings. You should be able to arrange information in order to make sense of it, for example, this could involve graphing information provided in a table. You must be able to analyse what information is being shown, for example, if the information shows an upward trend in the business performance. Or you must be able to examine the implications of a suggested idea or strategy.

There are revision sections thoughout this book that contain questions that give you practice of this skill.

The type of command words which are testing this area are: Analyse two factors…, Explain why…, Using accounting ratios, analyse…, Examine why the business…

Evaluation. This skill requires you to draw conclusions, make judgements or make recommendations, but they must be justified to ensure the marks are achieved, for example, 'Which would be the best form of finance for this business to use to pay for the expansion of its factory?' The question does not just test evaluation but also tests knowledge with understanding, application and some analysis. The mark scheme will reflect the different skills being tested and reward them accordingly.

Revision sections throughout this book contain questions that give you practice of this skill. Examiner's tips will also indicate where you need to include evaluation in your answers.

The type of command words which are testing this area are: Discuss…, Justify…, Consider…, Decide…, Which…, Evaluate…, Why do you think…, To what extent…, Do you agree…, Advise…, Assess…, Recommend…

As you work through the questions in this study guide, try to think about which skills the examiner is testing. For example, if the examiner is testing evaluation by asking if you agree with a particular proposal, then you must make judgements in your answer, so you should agree or disagree and explain why, otherwise you will not gain the higher marks.

Preparing for the examination

During the course

Preparing for an external examination is a continuous process throughout the course. All the activities, lessons, homework and assignments are major factors in determining your final examination grade, so the first piece of advice is to suggest that you work steadily throughout the one or two years of the course. It is essential that you prepare thoroughly for internal school examinations then, as you approach the IGCSE examination and start your revision programme, the topics will be familiar and the learning process will be less stressful and more productive. Revision should be what it says, refreshing your memory of what you need to know and be able to do for the examination; it should *not* be learning something for the first time.

Make sure that your notes are up to date. If you miss work through absence either copy it from a friend or leave a comment in your notes that will remind you to refer to the topic in a textbook. Similarly, look at any homework you have missed and if it involves the reinforcement of skills or concepts, then it would be a good idea to complete it.

In summary:

- work throughout the course
- ensure that your work is both complete and accurate
- learn the topics for tests and internal examinations
- seek assistance if you find an aspect of the course difficult.

Revision tips

- Divide your time so that you revise a section or topic at a time. You could do one unit from this guide at a time or you could group units together into the topic areas, for example, marketing would include Units 16 to 22.
- Learn the terms, concepts, facts, etc. thoroughly. Precise and clear answers are more likely to gain full marks. Vague answers may get some credit, but they are more likely to lose you marks.
- When you have learnt a particular topic practise answering the questions at the end of the units to test if you have learnt all the

information thoroughly. Pay particular attention to making sure you explain in detail.

Revision techniques

Well in advance of the examination, produce a revision timetable for all your subjects. Be realistic – you must include time for relaxation and socialising. Then create a more detailed timetable for Business Studies to cover all the topics. Ideally, you ought to go through the complete course twice. Keep a checklist of the topics studied – it is encouraging to have a visual record of your progress.

It is useful to have a syllabus, but not essential as this book includes all the information required for IGCSE Business Studies. You will need a quiet room at a comfortable temperature, plenty of paper and a pencil or biro. Some students find using highlighter pens helpful. On occasions revising with a friend makes a welcome and useful change. You will have to discover for yourself the length of time for which you can profitably study. This is a very individual characteristic and can vary from person to person – it may be as little as 30 minutes or over an hour. Do not exceed your optimum study time, break up the available time into study sessions and breaks. Introduce 'rewards' – when I have finished this section of work I will...

Revision must be active, so do not believe that just looking at a book is an effective way of learning. Your eyes can go over the words but the meaning never enters your brain! You can make flash cards that have bullet lists of essential points. You can study the topic for several minutes and then close the book and write out what you can remember – do not take great care over presentation – then check your account against the book. Repeat until you have most of the information correct, then move on to another section of the work.

This is the 'look, cover, write and check' technique and it is very effective for the majority of students. It is crucial that you repeat this technique on the same topic at least once, but preferably twice, soon after your first attempt, i.e. either later the same day or the next day.

Once you have acquired a reasonable knowledge of the course, it is time to extend the revision to practising on past papers. This is a most valuable form of preparation because not only does it provide a test of the effectiveness of your revision but it also provides an insight into what to expect in the 'real' examination. You need to practise the skills of application, analysis and evaluation. This requires you to look at case studies to answer questions. Paper 2 practice questions, in particular, will develop these skills but Paper 1 will ask questions in a business context and also develop these skills.

How to approach the examination

If your Centre or school has provided a detailed examination timetable, highlight your examinations and put this timetable in a prominent place in your home. Ask one of your parents to check with you each day so that you don't miss an examination.

Collect together the correct equipment the night before – pencil, pencil sharpener, eraser, ruler, calculator (are the batteries OK?) and two blue/black pens (in case one runs out).

Leave home in plenty of time. If you are late, you will not be given extra time and under certain circumstances you will not be allowed to enter the examination room. The regulations vary depending on the Examination Board. Do not put yourself at a disadvantage.

Advice for when you are about to take your external examinations

- Make sure you know the examination instructions. Read them on the front cover and obey them. Answer all the questions in the examination as there is no choice given.
- Read each question carefully and pay particular attention to the command words. Highlight or underline the key words in the question. Make sure you obey the command word, for example, if the question says 'state two examples' then don't explain them, but if it says 'explain…' then more than a simple statement is needed.
- Make sure you read a case study carefully and apply your answers in the context of the case study. This is especially important in questions where you are specifically asked to do so.
- Use all the information provided in the case study. Read the information carefully and underline key points.
- Do not repeat the same answer in different sections you do not usually gain double credit.
- Use the number of marks available for a question as a guide to the number of points needed if you are not told how many to include. Do not write a detailed answer to a question which is only worth 2 marks. However, if more marks are available then a detailed explanation will be needed. For questions using the command words for analysis and evaluation then fewer points will be required, but more in-depth discussion will be needed for the highest marks.
- Make sure you understand how to achieve the higher levels on a question where a level response mark scheme is used. These are usually the ones that are using the command words for analysis and evaluation and carry a relatively large number of marks, for example, 6, 8, 10, 12 marks. (Your teacher can explain this to you.)
- Be aware of the time available. Use your time wisely and don't spend a lot of time trying to answer questions you are not sure about. Answer the questions you are more confident in answering and go back to the other questions at the end of the examination. Also, if you have finished the examination before the end then re-read your answers and try to add to them. If you run out of space then fill any space underneath the question or answer on spare paper.
- Make sure the correct equipment is brought to the examination, such as pen, ruler, pencil, eraser and calculator.

After the examination the papers are sent to the examiner allocated to your Centre. This examiner will be part of a team headed by a Principal Examiner. All the members of the examining team will look at a sample of their scripts and assess the range of candidates' responses to each question. About a week after the examination, the team will meet to co-ordinate the marking for each question and decide the range of responses that are acceptable. During the marking period, the Principal Examiner will sample the marking of each examiner, at least twice, to ensure comparability of marking across the team. The scripts and the marks are returned to the Examination Board where the minimum mark for each grade is decided. A few weeks later you are informed of your grade.

How to improve your grade

Here are a few tips:

- Use this book. It was written to help students attain high grades.
- Learn all the work. Low grades are nearly always attributable to inadequate preparation. If you can recall the work, you will succeed and if you cannot, you will fail. Harsh, but true.
- Practise the skills necessary to be successful including calculations and interpretation of graphs.
- Make sure you can explain your answers in detail and do not make simple statements unless a question asks you for a simple statement.
- Use past papers to reinforce revision, to become familiar with the type of question, and to gain confidence.
- Answer the question on the examination paper – do not regard a question as an invitation to write about the topic.

Finally, good luck!

UNIT 1 The purpose of business activity

Key objectives

- To understand what is meant by scarcity
- To know what is meant by the economic problem
- To apply the idea of opportunity cost to a number of different situations
- To explain why specialisation is important in modern businesses
- To understand the nature of business activity and the groups involved in it

Key definitions

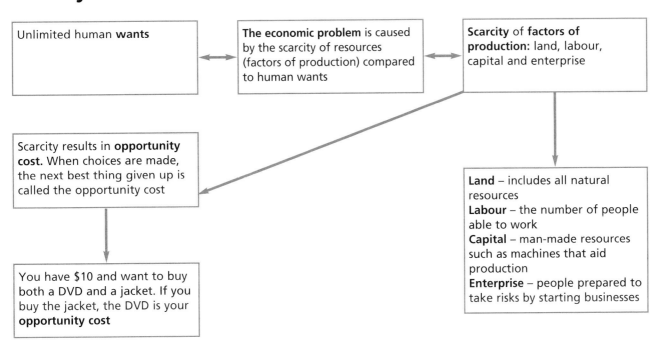

Term	Definition	Examples
Specialisation	Where resources are used to concentrate on producing one particular product.	Countries specialise, e.g. Qatar in oil production. Labour within a firm can specialise, too.
Division of labour	Each worker does one specialised job.	In a computer assembly factory each worker will perform a specialist task.
Business objectives	The targets or aims that a business is working towards.	Increase profits, increase sales, survive. Objectives can differ between businesses. The objectives of any one business can change over time, e.g. survival at start-up and profits once it is established.
Value added	The difference between the selling price of a product and the cost of the bought-in materials needed to make it.	If a firm sells a product for $15, but the materials that were bought in from other firms only cost $6, then the value added is $9.
Stakeholders	Groups of people with a direct interest in the performance of a business.	Workers, customers, consumers, shareholders, residents, government, banks. These groups often have different objectives for the business.

Sample questions and answers

Sample question The ARC Company produces and sells cosmetics for women and girls. The company is owned by a brother and sister. They wanted to make more money than they were earning in their old jobs. Although profitable, business sales have fallen in recent years. This is causing many stakeholder groups to worry about the future of the business. The owners are very keen for the business to continue. Sales are falling due to new competition in the market with exciting new products, so ARC must cut production costs to survive. The company has bought expensive new manufacturing equipment which is very specialised. Fewer workers are needed and they perform the same tasks each day and some workers have left because they are bored. Production has fallen as a result of this and ARC cannot supply all of the shops.

The marketing director is keen to increase the value added of the cosmetics. One product – the 'Bella' perfume – currently sells for $7. It is made from soap bought in by the business at a cost of $2 per item. The director believes that by designing new luxury packaging for the product, value added could be increased.

a) How do the business's objectives seem to have changed recently? [5 marks]

Marks *1 mark for explaining what a business objective is; 2 marks for identifying and explaining the original objective; 2 marks for identifying and explaining the more recent objective.*

Student's answer Most businesses have objectives that they aim for. The objective of this business is to survive. It has a lot of new competitors and sales are falling. Stakeholders are worried that the business might not survive so this is now the business's objective.

Examiner's marks and comments *The student understands that objectives are targets to aim for – 1 mark. The answer states that the latest objective is probably survival and explains why – 2 marks. However, there is no attempt to identify or explain the original objective that seems to have been profit. 3/5 marks.*

b) Explain the advantages and disadvantages of using division of labour for this business. [7 marks]

Marks *1 mark for explaining division of labour; 3 marks for explaining two or more advantages for this business (maximum 2 marks if no reference to this business); 3 marks for explaining two or more disadvantages for this business (maximum 2 marks if no reference to this business).*

Student's answer Division of labour is where a product is made by workers specialising on one stage of production each. The new machinery that ARC bought allowed the business to use division of labour. This means that each worker does what they are best at. This should increase output and improve quality. ARC should benefit from lower costs and this will help the business survive. However, division of labour does have its problems. The work can be boring as workers are only doing one job all the time.

Try to mark this yourself — the examiner's marks and comments are on page 99.

c) Assume that the marketing director bought in new packaging for the Bella perfume. This costs an extra $1 per unit. She increases the selling price by 20%. Calculate the new value added of this product. [3 marks]

Marks *If the candidate calculates the correct answer of $5.40 = 3 marks even with no working; if new bought-in costs of $3 is stated = 1 mark; if new selling price of $8.40 = 1 mark; if formula of value added is correctly given = 1 mark.*

Student's answer Value added = selling price less bought-in costs
= $7 + 20% less $3
= $8.40 less $3
= $5.40

Examiner's marks and comments *3 marks — well done!*

d) Evaluate any *one* alternative method that the marketing director could use to increase the value added of this product. [5 marks]

Marks *1 mark for identifying one other method; 2 marks for explaining how it might increase value added; 2 marks for evaluating this method.*

Student's answer To increase value added, the marketing director could keep the price the same but lower bought-in costs. Cheaper materials could be bought in for the perfume so that it does not cost so much to make. This will mean that value added from each bottle of perfume will rise.

However, cheaper materials might lead to lower quality. It might make the perfume smell differently. This could lead to fewer sales of the product. If consumers are looking for a quality product in this market then sales could be hit badly.

Try to mark this answer yourself — the examiner's marks and comments are on page 99.

Common misconceptions and errors

Error	Why it is wrong
'More money will solve the economic problem.'	The economic problem results from scarcity of resources rather than money.
'Stakeholders are the same as shareholders.'	Shareholders are just one group of stakeholders – there are other groups, too.
'Value added is the profit made on each unit.'	Value added is not profit as only the cost of bought-in materials/ components have been subtracted from the selling price.

● **Try this** A new plastics factory is to be built in your country. It will employ many workers and will export some of its output to other countries. It will be built on farmland several kilometres away from the main city. Other plastics businesses are worried about the competition it will bring. It could lead to lower prices for plastic products. Local residents have mixed feelings about the plan. The factory will use specialised equipment to allow for division of labour.

a) Identify four stakeholder groups that will be affected by the plan to build this new factory. [4 marks]

b) Discuss how two of these groups might be affected by the new factory. [8 marks]

Examiner's tip
✓ *You ought to try to think of how stakeholders might be affected in both positive and negative ways.*

c) Assess the effect on workers of using division of labour in the new factory. [8 marks]

Examiner's tip
✓ *Define division of labour and consider both advantages and disadvantages to workers.*

UNIT 2 Types of business activity

Key objectives

- To know the difference between the three stages of production: primary, secondary and tertiary
- To understand the difference between the private and public sectors of industry
- To explain the differences between horizontal, vertical and conglomerate mergers and takeovers
- To understand the different ways of measuring business size
- To explain why some businesses remain small

Key definitions

Types of business mergers and takeovers (integration) – an example from the oil industry:

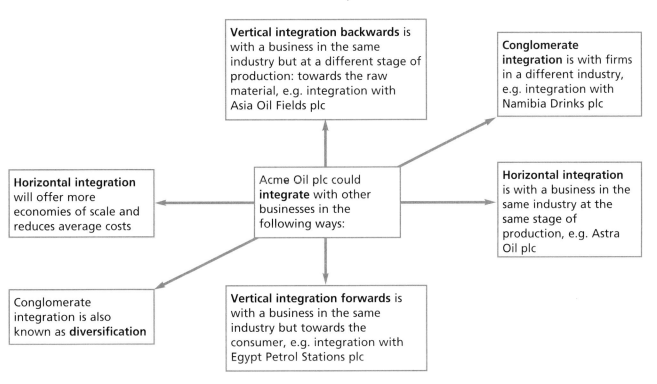

Vertical integration backwards is with a business in the same industry but at a different stage of production: towards the raw material, e.g. integration with Asia Oil Fields plc

Conglomerate integration is with firms in a different industry, e.g. integration with Namibia Drinks plc

Acme Oil plc could **integrate** with other businesses in the following ways:

Horizontal integration will offer more economies of scale and reduces average costs

Horizontal integration is with a business in the same industry at the same stage of production, e.g. Astra Oil plc

Conglomerate integration is also known as **diversification**

Vertical integration forwards is with a business in the same industry but towards the consumer, e.g. integration with Egypt Petrol Stations plc

Term	Definition	Examples
Primary production	Industries that extract and exploit the natural resources of the earth.	Mining, agriculture, forestry and fishing.
Secondary production	Industries that manufacture goods made from the raw materials provided by the primary sector.	Car production, computer assembly, food canning and steel making.
Tertiary production	Industries that provide services to consumers and other sectors of industry.	Travel agents, banking, insurance, health services and transport.
De-industrialisation	Relative decline in the importance of a country's secondary (manufacturing) sector.	Most advanced industrialised economies are experiencing this.

Term	Definition	Examples
Public sector	The sector of the economy in which organisations are owned and controlled by the state (government).	In most mixed economies, health services and railway services are in the public sector.
Private sector	The sector of the economy in which organisations are owned and controlled by individuals.	In most mixed economies, retailing and farming businesses are in the private sector.
Free market economy	All resources are privately owned. Prices are determined by supply and demand.	There are no 'pure' free market economies but the USA and South Korea, for example, have very large private sectors compared to the whole economy.
Planned economy	All resources are owned by the government, which also takes all major economic decisions.	Former communist countries in Eastern Europe had planned (or command) economies.
Mixed economy	Has both a private and a public sector.	Nearly all countries have mixed economies, but the balance between private and public sectors is not always the same.
Privatisation	The sale of state-owned assets such as public corporations to the private sector.	In many countries, for example, the UK and Germany, water, telephone and electricity industries have been privatised.
Capital-intensive businesses	Use a high proportion of capital equipment to produce their output.	Nuclear power plants, large automated car factories.
Labour-intensive businesses	Use a high proportion of labour to produce their output.	Fruit picking, private schools, call centres.
Internal growth	Business growth achieved by expanding the existing business.	Retailer opening a new shop, car factory extending to raise capacity.
External growth	Business growth achieved by merging with or taking over other businesses.	Hewlett Packard taking over Compaq computers, Chrysler merging with Daimler.

Sample questions and answers

Sample question   The main airline in Country X, Airco, is owned and managed by the central government.

a) The government decides to privatise this airline. Explain what this means. [2 marks]

Marks   *Up to 2 marks for brief explanation.*

Student's answer   This means that the government will sell the public sector airline to the private sector, perhaps to an existing private sector airline company.

Examiner's marks and comments   *Full marks for clear understanding – there was no need to add 'perhaps to an existing private sector airline company' but it was a good development.*

b) Which sector of industry is this business in? Justify your answer. [2 marks]

Marks   *1 mark for tertiary and 1 mark for brief explanation.*

Student's answer   The airline is in the secondary sector as it produces flights for passengers.

Examiner's marks and comments   *No, this is wrong so no marks. Airlines provide transport services to people and businesses so it is in the tertiary sector.*

c) Briefly analyse one argument for and one against the privatisation.   [4 marks]

Marks   *Up to 2 marks for each argument.*

Student's answer   By privatising the airline, the government will force it to become more efficient. It will have to compete with other airlines and will no longer be supported by the government. However, some flights might be stopped if they do not make enough profit. This will be a problem for the people affected.

Examiner's marks and comments   *Full marks as there are two clear arguments – one for and one against. The student has not wasted any time – the explanations are short and clear.*

d) An existing private sector airline, Airgroup, is interested in buying Airco from the government. This integration would make a much larger business. It would be one of the largest in the industry. The government is asking a high price for Airco and some staff do not want to leave the public sector.
   i) If this integration went ahead, would it be vertical, horizontal or conglomerate? Explain your answer.   [3 marks]

Marks   *1 mark for horizontal and up to 2 marks for explanation.*

Student's answer   This would be horizontal integration. This is because the two firms both provide services and are in the same industry.

Examiner's marks and comments   *2 marks for this answer because the explanation lacked detail – it should have gone on to say 'they are at the same stage of providing airline services'.*

   ii) Do you think it is likely to be a good idea for Airgroup to integrate with Airco? Justify your answer.   [8 marks]

Marks   *Up to 3 marks each for two explained advantages applied to this business (maximum 1 mark each if not applied) plus 2 marks for some judgement or evaluation.*

Student's answer   Airgroup might benefit in several ways from this takeover. It will reduce the number of competing airlines. This will reduce competition. Airgroup might be able to increase its prices because of this. Also, it might be able to buy aircraft more cheaply as there might be economies of scale because the firm is now much larger than before. So Airgroup will, therefore, definitely benefit from this takeover.

Try to mark this yourself – the examiner's marks and comments are on page 99.

Common misconceptions and errors

Error	Why it is wrong
'Organisations in the public sector include public limited companies.'	Public limited companies are in the private sector of industry (see Unit 3).
'There is both backward and forward horizontal integration.'	Horizontal integration is just between two firms at the same stage of production in the same industry; vertical integration can be either backwards or forwards.
'Profits are a good way of comparing the size of businesses.'	Profit levels can vary greatly between companies even if they are of similar size in terms of workers, capital, etc. Profits are not a good way of comparing business size.

● **Try this**

The table below shows some data for three shoe manufacturers in 2005.

	Sales turnover ($m)	Capital employed ($m)	Workers employed
Company X	160	35	1,500
Company Y	100	4	2,500
Company Z	50	10	700

a) Which is the largest business:
   i) in terms of sales? [1 mark]
   ii) in terms of capital employed? [1 mark]

b) How would you explain the high number of workers employed by Company Y yet the relatively low sales compared to Company X?
   [4 marks]

c) Company Z has not expanded in recent years. Explain any two possible reasons why this business remains quite small. [4 marks]

d) The directors of Company X are planning to take over a leather supplier. This will cost $10m. The directors expect the business to gain great advantages from this integration.
   i) What type of integration is this? Explain your answer. [3 marks]
   ii) Analyse *two* possible benefits to Company X from this integration.
      [4 marks]

e) The directors of Company Y are planning a merger with a chain of retail shoe shops. These shops currently sell a wide range of shoes from different manufacturers. Which sector of industry do the following businesses operate in?
   i) The shoe manufacturer, Company Y.
   ii) The retail shoe shops.

   In each case, explain your answer briefly. [4 marks]

    iii) Analyse *one* possible benefit to Company Y resulting from this
        integration.   [5 marks]

f) Do you think shoe retailers should be in the public or private sector
    in your country? Justify your answer.   [5 marks]

Examiner's tip
✓ *Define both sectors and then explain your opinion.*

9

UNIT 3 Forms of business organisation

Key objectives

- To understand the differences between limited and unlimited liability businesses
- To know the reasons why business owners choose to use different forms of business organisation
- To explain the differences between organisations in the private sector and organisations in the public sector
- To explain the advantages and disadvantages of all of these different forms of business organisation
- To evaluate these forms of business organisation in different circumstances

Key definitions

Sole trader: a business owned and operated by one person

Partnership: a business owned by 2–20 people

Types of business organisations

Public limited company: a business owned by shareholders that can sell shares to the public through the Stock Exchange. Remember: public limited companies are in the **private sector**

Public corporation: a business owned and controlled by the state – also known as nationalised industry. Remember: public corporations are in the **public sector**

Private limited company: a business owned by shareholders which cannot sell shares through the Stock Exchange

Term	Definition	Examples
Limited liability	The liability of the owners for the debts of the business is limited to the owners' investment.	Shareholders in all companies have limited liability.
Articles of Association	A legal document that must be completed before a business is given company status. It provides details of the internal rules of the company.	The issuing of shares and the rights and duties of directors.
Memorandum of Association	A legal document that must be completed before a business is given company status. It provides important information for shareholders.	The name, address, registered office and issued capital of the business. The objectives of the business are also stated.
Annual General Meeting (AGM)	Companies must hold these each year.	All shareholders have the right to attend and vote on which directors should run the company.
Co-operative	An organisation run by a group of people, each of whom has a financial interest in its success and a say in how it is managed.	Farmers in many countries operate as a co-operative to sell their produce.
Franchise	A business that uses the name, promotional logos and trading methods of an existing successful business.	McDonalds, Pizza Hut and Body Shop – most of their outlets are franchises owned by different people.

Sample questions and answers

Sample question Rashid has just left school. He wants to set up his own business as a gardener. Rashid wants to be able to control his own working life. He has very few savings – just enough to buy tools. He believes that he will need extra finance.

a) Briefly explain *two* benefits that Rashid could gain from setting up his own business. [4 marks]

Marks *1 mark for each benefit plus a further 1 mark each for some explanation.*

Student's answer If Rashid set up his own business, he would be working for himself. He could take all of his own decisions and would be independent. This seems to be important to him.
He could keep all of the profits from the business. This will encourage him to work hard to make his business a success.

Examiner's marks and comments *Full marks – two points made with brief explanation.*

b) What form of business organisation would you recommend Rashid to use? Explain your answer. [5 marks]

Marks *1 mark for correct identification of appropriate business form (for example, sole trader but accept partnership and private limited company if these are explained); 2 × 2 marks for two points well developed and applied to Rashid.*

Student's answer I would advise him to become a sole trader. These businesses are easy to set up with no expensive legal costs. There are no other owners, so all decisions can be taken by the owner.

Examiner's marks and comments *1 mark for referring to sole trader plus 2 marks for two advantages given. However, these are not applied to Rashid at all. For example, the student could have referred to Rashid's lack of finance (he may want to avoid legal costs) and his wish to take his own decisions. Therefore, no application marks. Total = 3/5 marks.*

c) Outline *two* other sources of finance that Rashid could use apart from his own savings. [4 marks]

Marks *1 mark for each appropriate source plus 1 extra mark for each explanation in the context of Rashid's business.*

Student's answer If Rashid does set up as a sole trader, he will have few sources of finance. He could ask a bank for a loan, but he will need to convince the bank that his business plan for gardening services is a good one. Once he has started working, he could use any profits that he makes to finance the business, but at the start there would not be any.

Examiner's marks and comments *Full marks as two sources are identified and explained in terms of Rashid's new business.*

d) After several months, Rashid has too much work! His business has been very successful in attracting new customers. He also has much work to do in his office such as keeping accounts and ordering supplies. A friend of Rashid's, Salman, is keen to become a partner and is taking accounting examinations, but he does not enjoy manual work. Salman has offered to invest some of his savings into the business so that some modern garden machinery can be bought. This would save Rashid a lot of time on some jobs.

Would you advise Rashid to take Salman as a partner in his business? Justify your answer. [8 marks]

Marks *2 marks for content of advantages/disadvantages of partnership; 2 marks for applying to Rashid's case; 2 marks for analysing at least one point in detail; 2 marks for discussion showing judgement.*

Student's answer If Rashid took Salman as a partner, he could share some of the work of running the business. Salman could do the accounts and Rashid could concentrate on the gardening. Salman could also put capital into the business. This would allow Rashid to buy equipment which would help him in his work.

However, Rashid would no longer be in full control and that is what he wanted. He would probably have to ask Salman before making big decisions, which would slow the process down.

I think that Rashid should take Salman as a partner. The business will then expand, but they should sign a Deed of Partnership to reduce the chance of arguments.

Try to mark this yourself – the examiner's marks and comments are on *page 100.*

Common misconceptions and errors

Error	Why it is wrong
'Sole traders can never employ other workers.'	The ownership and business control are in the hands of one person – this does not stop the sole trader from employing additional staff.
'All partners have to work in the business.'	Some partners can choose to take an active part in control of the business – this would need to be made clear in the Deed of Partnership. You can also have sleeping partners.
'A limited company can sell shares through the Stock Exchange.'	Only public limited companies (plc) can do this; private limited companies (Ltd) are restricted in who they can sell shares to.
'Public limited companies are in the public sector of industry.'	All private and public limited companies are in the private sector owned by private individuals; public corporations are owned by the government and are in the public sector.

● **Try this**

The growth of Onyema's cleaning business had surprised him. Starting just three years ago with a bucket and some sponges, he had offered cleaning services to local shops and offices. Within two months he had taken on three staff and his sister, Olena, as a partner. Further orders came flooding in from a wide range of businesses. Onyema and his sister decided one year ago to set up a private limited company. O and O Cleaning Ltd sounded impressive and it meant that the business would survive the death of either Onyema or Olena. They were keen to control their own business. However, they had further expansion plans. They wanted to set up franchised businesses in all regions and would supply the company name, logo, training and some cleaning equipment. This would need additional finance. The company accountant advised that the business should become a public limited company. Onyema and Olena had come a long way in three short years – were they ready for this huge step?

a) Outline *two* possible reasons why Onyema encouraged his sister to become a business partner.   [4 marks]

b) Explain what you understand by 'franchising'.   [2 marks]

c) Onyema and Olena decided to expand the business by offering franchises. Do you think this was a wise decision? Explain your answer.
                                                                         [6 marks]

Examiner's tip
✓ *Give the advantages and disadvantages of franchising before deciding.*

d) Imagine that you plan to open an 'O and O Cleaning' franchise. Explain the advantages of this plan rather than setting up a new cleaning business.   [6 marks]

e) Outline *two* differences between a private limited company and a public limited company.   [4 marks]

f) Would you recommend Onyema and Olena to convert their company into a public limited company? Justify your answer.   [8 marks]

Examiner's tip
✓ *Explain the advantages and disadvantages before making your recommendation.*

UNIT 4 Government and economic influences on business

Key objectives

- To explain why and how governments control business activity
- To explain why and how governments support business
- To know the economic objectives of governments
- To understand the measures that governments can take to control the economy
- To understand the impact of business activity on society

Key definitions

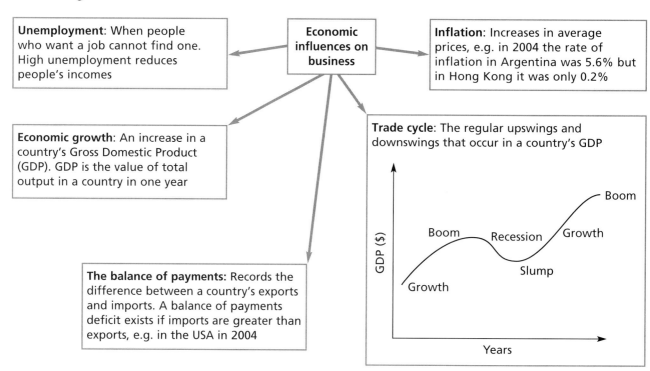

Unemployment: When people who want a job cannot find one. High unemployment reduces people's incomes

Economic influences on business

Inflation: Increases in average prices, e.g. in 2004 the rate of inflation in Argentina was 5.6% but in Hong Kong it was only 0.2%

Economic growth: An increase in a country's Gross Domestic Product (GDP). GDP is the value of total output in a country in one year

The balance of payments: Records the difference between a country's exports and imports. A balance of payments deficit exists if imports are greater than exports, e.g. in the USA in 2004

Trade cycle: The regular upswings and downswings that occur in a country's GDP

Term	Definition	Examples
Exports	Goods and services sold by a country to other countries.	Cotton goods are one of Egypt's major exports.
Imports	Goods and services bought by one country from other countries.	Argentina has to import oil and gas.
An increase in real income	When income rises at a faster rate than inflation.	If an individual's income rises by 5% per year and prices rise by 3% then real income has increased by 2%.
Recession	A period when a country's GDP is falling.	Japan's GDP (after inflation) fell by 1% in 2002.
Economic boom	A period of very fast economic growth which can lead to high inflation.	China's economy grew by 8% in 2003.
Exchange rate	The price of one currency in terms of another.	1 US$:1 euro.

Term	Definition	Examples
Exchange rate depreciation	A fall in the exchange rate of a currency.	If the exchange rate for the US$ fell from 1 US$:1 euro to 1 US$:0.6 euro then the US$ has depreciated.
Direct taxes	Paid directly from incomes.	Income tax, company profits tax.
Indirect taxes	Taxes on goods and services.	Value added tax, duties on petrol and alcohol.
Import tariff	A tax on imported goods to discourage their sale.	Malaysia has a 200% tariff on imported cars.
Import quota	A legal limit on the quantity of a product that may be imported.	The EU used to place quotas on imported Japanese cars.
Consumer protection laws	Laws designed to protect consumers from unfair actions by producers or retailers.	UK Consumer Credit Act 2004.
Monopoly	A business that has no competition in its market – it is the sole seller.	Microsoft has 95% of the market for computer operating systems.
Illegal discrimination	Unfavourable treatment of someone on specific grounds, unrelated to their ability to do the job.	Not recruiting a person because of their age, gender, race, religion, sexuality, or because they have a disability.
Ethical decision	A decision taken on moral grounds.	A soft drink firm deciding to stop advertising directly to children as the drinks could be one of the causes of tooth decay in children.
Contract of employment	A legal agreement between workers and employers listing the rights and responsibilities of employees.	It will include hours of work, holiday allowance, expected levels of behaviour, pension benefits.
National minimum wage	The legal minimum hourly wage rate.	In the UK in 2004 this was set at £4.85 per hour.

Sample questions and answers

Sample question Fogla's is a supermarket that sells a variety of food and household products. It pays most of its workers the national minimum wage. The company imports many food products from other countries. The manager of Fogla's decided to open a café within the supermarket, which is proving to be popular. It sells quite expensive meals and drinks, but the average income of local residents is high.

a) Explain one likely reason why the government insists on a national minimum wage. [4 marks]

Marks *1 mark for suggesting a likely reason; 1–3 marks for detailed development.*

Student's answer The government might have wanted to protect workers. When there are not many jobs, employers might try to pay workers as little as possible. They could take advantage of workers and only pay them very low wages. Workers would have to accept the jobs. The government wants to prevent workers from being exploited.

Examiner's marks and comments *This is a good answer. A clear reason is given. This is then developed and explained in enough detail. 4 marks.*

b) The government plans to increase the national minimum wage by 20%. Discuss the likely effects of this decision on Fogla's.

[8 marks]

Marks *2 marks for knowledge of two effects; 2 marks for applying these to this business; 2 marks for analysis of these effects; 2 marks for some discussion and judgement.*

Student's answer Fogla's will have to pay higher wages to many of its workers. This will raise the firm's costs. The company's profits could fall. The manager of the supermarket might even make some workers redundant to save costs, so the effect is likely to be bad. Workers in other businesses will also have higher wages and more money to spend though.

Examiner's marks and comments *2 marks awarded for knowledge (higher costs for Fogla's and higher incomes for other workers); 1 mark for some application; 1 mark for explaining the impact of higher costs (possibly lower profits). Total = 4/8 marks. The student did not analyse the second point and there was no evaluation of the possible positive impact of higher wages on the business. For example, higher wages could increase incomes for workers in other businesses and this could lead to higher spending and increased sales for Fogla's.*

c) Analyse the likely effect on Fogla's of a depreciation in the country's foreign exchange rate. [6 marks]

Marks *Up to 3 knowledge marks for good understanding of exchange rates and depreciation; up to 3 analysis marks for explaining the impact on this business.*

Student's answer A depreciation of a country's exchange rate means that its currency is worth less. For example, if the value of $1 falls from £2 to £1.50 then the $ value has depreciated. The exchange rate is the price of one currency measured against another. This depreciation will make imports more expensive. Goods bought from other countries will be more expensive. Fogla's prices might be higher than other supermarkets that do not import.

Examiner's marks and comments *This shows real understanding. The student also analyses the effect of a depreciation on Fogla's accurately. Full marks.*

d) Fogla's manager is worried when he sees the following newspaper headline:

INTEREST RATES SET TO RISE TO SLOW DOWN INFLATION

Discuss the likely effects of higher interest rates on Fogla's profits.

[8 marks]

Marks *Up to 2 marks for knowledge shown about interest rates and inflation; 2 marks for analysing the effects on business; 2 marks for applying these effects to Fogla's; 2 marks for some discussion/judgement.*

Student's answer   Inflation is when prices rise, and interest rates are the cost of borrowing money. Higher interest rates will affect Fogla's in several ways. It will cost the firm more to borrow. This could mean that it decides not to expand. Also, higher interest rates will mean that consumers will have less to spend. They might not go to Fogla's café so often, especially because it is quite expensive. On the other hand, Fogla's might not be much affected. It mainly sells food, and consumers will still need to buy this no matter how high interest rates are. Also, if inflation does fall because of higher interest rates then the firm's costs will not rise so quickly. There will, therefore, be some positive and some negative effects.

Try to mark this yourself – the examiner's marks and comments are on page 100.

Try to mark this yourself – the examiner's marks and comments are on page 100.

Common misconceptions and errors

Error	Why it is wrong
'Economic booms are always good for the economy.'	They can lead to higher incomes, but 'booms' can lead to high inflation and lower levels of output eventually.
'Inflation means the economy is expanding.'	Inflation is the measure of the rate of price increases.
'A recession will lead to a fall in demand for all goods.'	A recession lowers consumers' incomes – they could switch to buying cheaper goods so the demand for these could rise.
'An exchange rate depreciation means the value of the country's currency has risen.'	No – it has fallen in terms of other currencies.
'An exchange rate appreciation will make exports cheaper.'	Exports rise in price after an appreciation of the currency.

● **Try this**   Mim Chul Ltd produces soft drinks based on fresh fruit. The company has a monopoly in Country X. The drinks are advertised to consumers with the slogan 'Drink Mim Chul's juices and you will never be ill'.

a) Explain the term 'monopoly'.   [2 marks]

b) Explain why the government might decide to protect the consumers of soft drinks in Country X.   [6 marks]

Examiner's tip
✓ *You could write about the firm's monopoly position and the advertising it uses.*

---

c) The company plans to build a new factory to make the drinks. It wants to build on a site close to houses and schools. The government has planning controls over the building of new factories. Mim Chul Ltd has a poor reputation for health and safety in its factories.

Outline *one* possible reason why the government has planning controls for the building of new factories. [4 marks]

d) The government has offered Mim Chul's business a grant for the new factory if it is built in another area. From the following list, place a tick alongside the *two* most likely reasons for this. [2 marks]

Possible reason for government grant
To increase imports
To create more jobs
To increase inflation
To increase demand for the products of local suppliers

e) Discuss whether Mim Chul Ltd should spend money on improving health and safety in its factories. [8 marks]

Examiner's tip

✓ *Think about the disadvantages of not having good working conditions.*

UNIT 5 Other external influences on business

Key objectives

- To understand the other external constraints that affect business activity
- To recognise how technology can affect businesses
- To know why the environment is of increasing concern to most businesses
- To understand how cost benefit analysis can be used to measure the full social costs and benefits of business decisions

Key definitions

Term	Definition	Examples
Technological change	Changes in products or the ways products are made resulting from research into new ideas.	Mobile phones with cameras. Robots used to make cars.
Pressure groups	Groups of people who share a common interest and take action to achieve the changes they are seeking.	Trade unions, Greenpeace, World Wide Fund for Nature.
Private costs	The costs to producers and consumers of an economic activity.	The costs paid for by a chemical firm when producing products.
External costs	The costs of an economic activity paid for by the rest of society, not the producers/consumers.	Pollution from a chemical factory which harms the environment and may damage the health of local residents.
Private benefits	The benefits of an economic activity to producers/consumers.	The benefit to a driver of using a car.
External benefits	The benefits of an economic activity received by the rest of society other than producers/consumers.	A new airport may encourage tourists to a region, which will bring jobs to firms other than the airport.
Cost benefit analysis	An analysis, usually carried out by the government, into the overall costs and benefits (private and external) of a large new project.	An analysis of the impact of a new motorway on users, residents, road safety, etc.

Sample questions and answers

Sample question Norris Cars Ltd manufactures hand-built sports cars. The business has a huge customer waiting list. The directors have decided to make a new model of a car using the latest production technology. Workers who have used the same methods for many years will have to learn new skills. The new machines will cut down on waste materials and pollution from the factory. Residents have often complained to the local government about Norris Cars and the external costs caused by the factory.

a) Using an example, explain what is meant by the term 'external costs'.   [3 marks]

Marks *Up to 2 marks for an understanding of this term plus 1 mark for an appropriate example.*

Student's answer External costs are when people other than the producer or consumer of a good or service have to pay the costs of producing a product. An example is the pollution from a factory that society has to pay to be cleaned up.

Examiner's marks and comments *Full marks – good definition and relevant example.*

b) The following list gives the possible effects of the decision by Norris Cars to purchase the latest technology equipment. Identify with a PC, EC, PB or EB whether they are private or external costs or benefits. [4 marks]

Cost or benefit	Private or external cost/benefit
Higher profits if production costs are lowered	
Jobs may be lost if the machines are much more efficient	
Pollution and waste will be reduced	
Training costs will be high	

Marks *1 mark for each correct answer.*

Student's answer

Cost or benefit	Private or external cost/benefit
Higher profits if production costs are lowered	PB
Jobs may be lost if the machines are much more efficient	EC
Pollution and waste will be reduced	EB
Training costs will be high	PC

Examiner's marks and comments *4 marks for correct answers.*

c) Do you think that the workers at Norris Cars Ltd would think the purchase of the new machinery was a good idea or not? Explain your answer. [8 marks]

Marks *Up to 2 marks for identifying relevant factors; up to 2 marks for applying these to this business; up to 2 marks for analysing at least one of these points; up to 2 marks for some judgement/evaluation.*

Student's answer The case tells us that workers will need to be retrained. Some will be afraid of this. They may have done the same job for years and this could mean they do not want to learn new skills, or they might be slow learners. This uncertainty could reduce their job security and motivation so that they do not work as hard as they could. It is likely, therefore, that they will not think that it is a good idea.

Examiner's marks and comments *1 mark for content as only one factor was mentioned; 1 mark for application; 2 marks for analysis as the impact on motivation is explained; 1 mark for very limited evaluation. The answer could have been improved by considering one other factor – workers will now be multi-skilled and will be more able to find other jobs if they wanted to. Total = 5/8 marks.*

Common misconceptions and errors

Error	Why it is wrong
'New technology always leads to unemployment.'	New technology can create jobs, as people need to make and service the new machinery. New technology also creates new products and new markets.
'Workers will always be opposed to technological change.'	Some workers will become more skilled, which would increase their chances of gaining other jobs. Technology could make jobs more secure if the firm becomes more efficient.
'Cost benefit analysis measures the profit of a project.'	Cost benefit analysis tries to assess both private and external costs and benefits (social costs and benefits) – it is not concerned with profit.

● Try this Here is a recent newspaper article:

GOVERNMENT PLANS NEW AIRPORT IN NORTH WEST

Central Government intends to allow a large new airport to be built in the North West. This is an area of high unemployment and more flights into the area will lead to more tourists and increased exports. It is also hoped that new companies will be set up as the North West will now be cheaper for the transportation of goods. Many local residents are totally opposed to the idea of the new airport. They have formed a pressure group called 'SANW' (Stop Airport in North West). Most local firms have welcomed the new airport plan. However, some business people in the area are worried about increased competition and a possible shortage of skilled labour. The local government authority is hoping that its tax revenues will rise from airport charges, but it is worried about the effect on local pollution levels.

---

a) What do you understand by the term 'pressure group'? [2 marks]

b) List A (below) shows the stakeholders affected by the government's decision. Identify the major impact on each group from List B. [9 marks]

21 ●

List A	List B
Central Government	Increased local tax payments
Local workers in employment	Noise from aircraft
Local government authority	More choice of jobs for skilled workers
Residents living close to the new airport	Increased competition from airlines
Local unemployed workers	More chance of finding a job
Businesses in the North West	Easier to import and export goods
Airlines	Increased exports from the economy
Train companies	Destruction of nature sites
Environmentalists	Increased flights mean expansion

c) Imagine that you are *either* a member of the SANW pressure group *or* a North West business owner. Write a letter to the Government explaining why you *either* oppose *or* support the new airport plan.   [10 marks]

Examiner's tip
✓ *Try to explain three separate points in your letter.*

UNIT 6 Business costs and revenue

Key objectives

- To know the difference between different kinds of costs
- To understand what 'break-even level of production' means
- To draw and analyse simple break-even charts
- To calculate the break-even point from data
- To know what a budget is and why budgeting is important
- To understand how economies of scale arise

Key definitions

Term	Definition	Examples/calculation	Diagram
Fixed costs	These costs do not vary with the number of items sold or produced.	Rent of building Interest on loans Managers' salaries	
Variable costs	These costs vary directly with the number of items sold or produced.	Cost of raw materials Electricity used for machinery Production labour costs	
Total cost	The addition of fixed and variable costs.	Total cost = Fixed costs + Variable costs	
Total revenue (Sales revenue)	The income of a business during a time period from the sale of output.	Total revenue = Quantity sold × Price	
Break-even chart	This is a graph which shows the costs and revenue of a business and the level of sales that must be made to break even.		
Break-even point	The level of sales or output at which Total costs = Total revenue.	See diagram above.	
Direct costs	These are costs that can be directly related to a particular product or department.	In a factory making clothes, leather used for making one style of coat is a direct cost.	
Indirect costs (also known as overheads)	These are costs that cannot be directly related to a particular product or department.	In a factory making clothing, electricity costs would be very difficult to 'divide' accurately between products and departments.	
Average costs (also known as unit costs)	These are the costs per unit of output.	Calculated by: $\dfrac{\text{Total costs}}{\text{Total output}}$ For example, if costs = \$30,000 and total output = 10,000 units, then average cost = \$3.	
Contribution	The contribution of a product is selling price less variable cost.	If a computer costs \$100 in materials and labour (variable costs), but is sold for \$250, then contribution is \$150.	
Budget	This is a plan for the future containing numerical or financial targets.	A budget for the marketing department might be '\$50,000 to be spent on promotion over the next 12 months'.	
Forecast	This is a prediction of the future, for example, sales forecast.	A firm forecasts that it will sell 200 units per month over the next year.	

Term	Definition	Examples/calculation
Economies of scale	These are the cost advantages of producing on a large scale.	Purchasing, marketing, and financial, managerial and technical economies.
Diseconomies of scale	These are the disadvantages of producing on a large scale.	Poor communication, low morale amongst workers.

Sample questions and answers

Sample question The Cairo Tyre Company has asked you to help with some costing problems. The manager, Mr Shah, does not know if the factory has reached break-even point. He is also unsure of the likely benefits that could be gained from expanding the business. He gives you the following information:

Annual fixed costs:	$50,000
Labour cost per tyre:	$1
Variable cost per tyre:	$2
Selling price to customers:	$5 per tyre

Last year, the marketing department spent much more than Mr Shah expected them to. This was one of the reasons why the company made a loss last year. Despite this, Mr Shah has plans to expand the factory as he believes that this would increase the chances of making profits in the future.

a) For this business, are labour and materials variable costs? Explain your answer. [4 marks]

Marks *1 mark for knowledge: What is meant by a variable cost? 1 mark for application to this business; 2 marks for explanation of why these costs are variable and not fixed costs.*

Student's answer Yes, labour and material costs are variable costs for the Cairo Tyre Company because they will change with the number of tyres made. The more tyres that are made, the more labour and materials will be needed to produce them. Therefore, as output of tyres increases, these costs will increase.

Examiner's marks and comments *The first sentence shows understanding that variable costs vary with output and the student also applied it to the case by mentioning the number of tyres made (2 marks). The second sentence explains clearly that these costs increase as the number of tyres produced increases (2 more marks). Total = 4 marks.*

b) Calculate the break-even level of output for this business – show all workings. [4 marks]

Marks *1 mark for break-even formula; 1 mark for contribution calculation; 1 mark for attempted break-even result (incorrect); 2 marks for correct break-even result.*

Student's answer The break-even level of output = $\dfrac{\text{Fixed costs}}{\text{Contribution per unit}}$

Contribution per unit = Selling price minus variable costs
= $5 − $3
= $2

The break-even level of output $= \dfrac{\$50,000}{\$2} = 25,000$ tyres

Examiner's marks and comments   *Full marks again for a correct answer — note how the working is clearly laid out, so even if a mistake had been made the examiner could still have given some marks for a correct method.*

c) Use the break-even chart below.

    i) Identify the break-even level of output on the graph and state what it is.   [2 marks]

    ii) What is the level of profit at an output level of 50,000 tyres?   [2 marks]

    iii) Explain what would happen to the break-even level of output if the price of tyres was raised to $7. State *one* assumption that you make.   [6 marks]

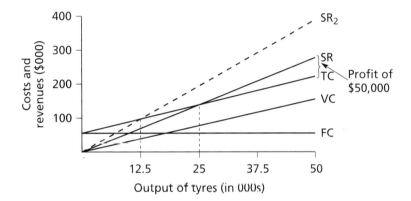

Marks   *1 mark for appropriate assumption; 1 mark for correct new revenue line; 2 marks for correct new break-even point; 2 marks for correct new profit figure.*

Student's answer   i) The break-even level of output is 25,000 tyres – I have shown this with a dotted line.

    ii) The profit made is $50,000 at an output of 50,000 tyres – I have shown this on the graph. It is the difference between sales revenue and total cost.

    iii) The new revenue line is the dotted line I have added (SR$_2$). The break-even point falls to 12,500 tyres. I have assumed that sales remain the same.

Examiner's marks and comments   *This answer gained full marks. The student correctly answered all parts of the question. The assumption about sales is important — if the price is raised and sales fall then the firm might not reach the break-even point.*

d) Explain briefly *two* economies of scale that the company might benefit from if it expanded.   [6 marks]

Marks   *1 mark for each correct example of an economy of scale; 2 marks for each economy that has been explained and applied to the case study.*

Student's answer   Economies of scale reduce average costs as a firm expands. Two examples are purchasing or bulk-buying economies and managerial economies. The tyre factory might be able to buy rubber more cheaply if it bought greater amounts, as it would receive a discount when placing bulk orders. Also, specialist managers could be recruited to manage the business more efficiently, for example, a specialist marketing manager to oversee the marketing of the tyres.

Examiner's marks and comments *Full marks – two good suggestions and both were accurately explained and applied.*

Common misconceptions and errors

Error	Why it is wrong
'Variable costs vary over time.'	Very common error. Variable costs vary with the level of output not with time.
'Fixed costs never change.'	Fixed costs may change in the long run if the firm expands its total capacity.
'Economies of scale reduce total costs.'	No – they do not reduce total costs. As a firm expands, total costs are likely to rise, but economies of scale could reduce average costs of production.
'Break even is the time it takes for a firm to cover all costs.'	The break-even point is measured in units of output/sales *not* time.
'Budgets are forecasts of what will happen in the future.'	Forecasts are predictions, but budgets are *plans*. A company needs to plan for the future and budgets are plans with financial targets.

● **Try this**

a) Indicate whether the following costs of a bakery business are direct or indirect costs by ticking the correct column. [4 marks]

Costs	Direct	Indirect
Flour		
Salary of office manager		
Wages of bakery workers		
Rent of the building		

b) Referring to the Cairo Tyre Company case above, explain to the manager the possible benefits to his business of using budgets for each department. [6 marks]

c) Outline *one* possible diseconomy of scale that the Cairo Tyre Company might experience if it expanded. [3 marks]

d) Do you think that break-even charts are a useful technique for managers to use? Explain your answer. [8 marks]

> **Examiner's tip**
> ✓ As well as explaining two advantages, also consider two possible drawbacks to break-even charts.

UNIT 7 Business accounting

Key objectives

- To understand why businesses keep accounting records and how they use them
- To analyse the needs of the different users of business accounts
- To understand the construction of simple balance sheets
- To understand the construction of simple profit and loss accounts
- To analyse business accounts using ratios

Key definitions

Term	Definition	Examples
Profit and loss account	An account that records business sales revenue, all costs and expenses, and any loss/profit made during the year. (N.B. Brackets round a number mean that it is a minus figure).	ABD Traders Ltd profit and loss account for year ending 31/9/04 ($) <table><tr><td>Sales turnover</td><td>12,000</td></tr><tr><td>Costs of goods sold</td><td>(4,000)</td></tr><tr><td>Gross profit</td><td>8,000</td></tr><tr><td>Overheads</td><td>(3,000)</td></tr><tr><td>Net profit</td><td>5,000</td></tr></table>
Trading account	The part of the profit and loss account that records revenue, cost of sales and gross profit.	
Sales turnover (Sales revenue)	The value of sales in a certain time period.	If 1200 items were sold for $10 each then the firm's sales revenue is $12,000.
Gross profit	Profit after subtracting the cost of sales from sales turnover.	If goods costing the firm $4,000 were sold for $12,000 then gross profit = $8,000.
Net profit	Profit after subtracting all expenses/overheads from gross profit.	If gross profit = $8,000 and the firm's expenses/overheads are $3,000 then net profit = $5,000.
Corporation tax	Tax on company net profits.	If this is at 40% and net profits are $5,000 then the company will pay $2,000 in corporation tax.
Dividends	Annual payments from company profits to shareholders.	
Depreciation	The fall in the value of fixed assets over time.	Machines and vehicles fall in value each year.
Liquidity	The ability of the business to convert its assets into cash and pay off short-term debts.	Calculated by using the next two ratios.
Current ratio	$\dfrac{\text{Current assets}}{\text{Current liabilities}}$	Using the balance sheet on page 28: $\dfrac{2{,}500}{1{,}700} = 1.47$
Acid test ratio	$\dfrac{\text{Current assets} - \text{Stock}}{\text{Current liabilities}}$	Using the balance sheet on page 28: $\dfrac{1{,}500}{1{,}700} = 0.88$
Return on capital employed (%)	$\dfrac{\text{Net profit}}{\text{Capital employed}} \times 100$	Using the accounts above and the balance sheet: $\dfrac{5{,}000}{19{,}800} \times 100 = 25.3\%$

Term	Definition	Examples
Retained profit (Reserves)	Profit made after payment of tax and dividends. It is reinvested back into the business.	
Gross profit margin (%)	$\dfrac{\text{Gross profit}}{\text{Sales turnover}} \times 100$	Using the accounts on page 27: $\dfrac{8{,}000}{12{,}000} \times 100 = 66.7\%$
Net profit margin (%)	$\dfrac{\text{Net profit}}{\text{Sales turnover}} \times 100$	Using the accounts on page 27: $\dfrac{5{,}000}{12{,}000} \times 100 = 41.7\%$
Balance sheet	The account records all business assets and liabilities and the value of shareholders' funds.	ABD Traders Ltd balance sheet for year ending 31/9/04 ($) (see below).
Working capital	The capital needed by a business to finance its day-to-day needs.	Using the balance sheet below: 800 – it is the same as the net current assets.
Fixed assets	Assets owned by a business that it expects to keep and use for more than one year.	Buildings, machinery and motor vehicles.
Current assets	Assets that the business will use up or turn into cash within one year.	Stocks, debtors, cash.
Current liabilities	Loans and debts of the business that will be repaid within one year.	Bank overdraft and creditors.
Long-term liabilities	The money value of debts that do not have to be repaid in one year.	Long-term loans and debentures.
Shareholders' funds	Finance provided by shareholders – share capital or retained profits.	Share capital is from sale of shares. Retained profits are called reserves.
Capital employed	Total value of business's long-term finance.	Long-term liabilities plus shareholders' funds.

Balance sheet:

Fixed assets:	
Buildings	13,000
Machinery	6,000
	19,000
Current assets:	
Stocks	1,000
Debtors	1,000
Cash	500
	2,500
Current liabilities:	
Overdraft	1,200
Creditors	500
	1,700
Net current assets	800
Total assets less current liabilities	**19,800**
Long-term liabilities:	
Loans	12,000
Shareholders' funds:	
Capital	5,000
Reserves	2,800
Capital employed	**19,800**

creditor – current liability. (公司 creditor账)

Sample questions and answers

Sample question

Table 1: Financial information about City Café Ltd ($000)

	2004	2005
Sales revenue	200	250
Net profit	25	15
Current liabilities	20	20
Current assets	50	20
Capital employed	300	300

a) State and explain *two* ways in which the owners of City Café Ltd might use the net profits of the business. [4 marks]

Marks *1 mark each for identifying the uses of net profit and 1 mark each for briefly explaining each use.*

Student's answer The owners of this business could use the net profits either to pay dividends or to keep in the business. Shareholders will expect some dividends as they have invested in the business. If profit is left in the business, it is called retained profit. This could be used for expansion.

Examiner's marks and comments *Very good answer – 4 marks. Two uses are identified and briefly explained.*

b) Using figures from Table 1 and a ratio, analyse the liquidity of the company. [5 marks]

Marks *1 mark for correctly writing down the current ratio; 2 marks for calculation (both years); up to 2 marks for explaining what the result shows about liquidity.*

Student's answer The current ratio is a liquidity ratio and uses this formula:

$$\frac{\text{Current assets}}{\text{Current liabilities}}$$

In 2004 the result was: $\frac{50}{20} = 2.5$ and in 2005 the result was: $\frac{20}{20} = 1$

This shows that the liquidity of the business is improving as 1 is a better result than 2.5. The firm will find it easier to pay its short-term debts.

Examiner's marks and comments *The student makes a good start by accurately stating the formula for the current ratio. The two calculations are correct. The rest of the answer is **wrong**, as the student does not understand what the current ratio result shows about liquidity. Liquidity has, of course, got worse from 2004 to 2005 and if this continues, the business will find it difficult to pay off its short-term liabilities. 3 marks.*

c) Using the figures in Table 1 and ratio analysis, evaluate the performance of the City Café Ltd between 2004 and 2005. [10 marks]

Marks *Up to 2 marks for correctly stating two relevant ratios, for example, net profit margin and return on capital employed. Up to 4 marks for calculations (both years). Up to 4 marks for discussion which analyses the results and draws a conclusion about the performance of the business.*

Student's answer

	2004	2005
Net profit margin = $\frac{\text{Net profit}}{\text{Sales}} \times 100$	12.5%	6%
Return on capital employed = $\frac{\text{Net profit}}{\text{Capital employed}} \times 100$	8.3%	5%

These results show that the profitability of the business is falling. The firm is making less profit per $ of sales, perhaps because costs are rising faster than price.

Return on capital employed has fallen which means that the money invested in the business is making less of a return.

Both of these figures are poor, but it would help if we had results from other café businesses to see if City Café is better or worse at making profits than they are.

Try to mark this yourself – the examiner's marks and comments are on page 101.

Common misconceptions and errors

Error	Why it is wrong
Not remembering the ratios.	Obvious! Use the list above to help you.
Putting sales revenue in the balance sheet.	This is a profit and loss account item – only assets and liabilities appear in the balance sheet.
'Any current ratio result below 1 means the firm is bankrupt.'	A result of 1 is acceptable – it means that all short-term debts are covered by current assets. Even below 1, a firm may be liquid enough as it is unlikely that it will have to repay *all* short-term debts at the same time.
'Gross profit is always less than net profit.'	Net profit is gross profit *after* expenses have been taken away, so net profit is always lower.
'Creditors owe the firm money.'	Debtors are customers who have not yet paid – they owe the firm money. The firm *owes* money to its creditors.

● **Try this**

The 2005 accounts for Titan Tankers plc have just been published. Groups of stakeholders in the business have been waiting to analyse these.

a) Identify *two* of the main accounts that will appear in these published accounts. [2 marks]

b) Explain what *one* of these accounts contains. [3 marks]

c) Table 1 contains a list of stakeholders in Titan Tankers plc who want to use and analyse the company accounts. Copy the table and fill in the 'Useful for' column with *one* of the options below:

Table 1: The users of published accounts

Stakeholders:	Useful for:
Shareholders	
Trade union	
Government	
Creditors	

Options:
i) seeing what the level of dividends will be this year

ii) analysing whether the business has sufficient liquidity

iii) seeing whether the business plans to expand or reduce the labour force

iv) assessing whether the business seems to be making excess profits.

[4 marks]

d) Using the figures in Table 2 and ratio analysis, evaluate the performance of this company over the last year. [10 marks]

Table 2: Financial information from Titan Tankers plc 2005 accounts ($000)

	2004	2005
Sales revenue	300	350
Gross profit	60	60
Net profit	30	25
Capital employed	200	240

Examiner's tip

✓ *Explain what your results indicate about the company's performance. Should these results be compared with any others?*

UNIT 8 Cash flow planning

Key objectives

- To understand what is meant by cash inflows, cash outflows and net cash flows
- To analyse a simple cash flow forecast
- To understand why such forecasts are helpful to businesses
- To explain how a business might deal with a cash flow problem

Key definitions

Cash inflow: The amount of cash received by a business in each time period

	All figs in $000
Cash inflow:	
Cash from sales	5,000
Cash outflow:	
Materials	1,000
Labour	1,500
Total cash outflow	2,500
Opening balance	1,000
Net cash flow	2,500
Closing balance	3,500

Cash outflow: The amount of cash paid out by a business over a period of time

Term	Definition	Example
Cash flow forecast	A table showing the estimated cash flows of a business over a time period. Such forecasts help to identify future finance problems and help the firm to plan for its cash needs.	See Table 1 on page 33.
Opening balance	The amount of cash the business holds at the start of a time period.	For the business in Table 1, the opening balance in October is $3,000.
Closing balance	The amount of cash held by a business at the end of a time period.	Opening balance $15,000. Monthly net cash flow $4,000. Closing balance = $19,000.
Cash flow cycle	This shows the stages between a business paying out for materials, labour and other costs and receiving cash from the sale of goods. The cash flow cycle	See the cash flow cycle figure below.

The cash flow cycle: 1 Cash needed to pay for → 2 Materials, wages, rent, etc. → 3 Goods produced → 4 Goods sold → 5 Cash payment received for goods sold → (back to 1)

Term	Definition	Example
Liquidity crisis	When a business does not have enough cash to pay immediate debts.	If a firm is short of cash, it may have to arrange a bank overdraft or other loans to meet immediate debts.

Sample questions and answers

Sample question Zippo Printers Ltd publishes a range of books, calendars and birthday cards. The directors are planning an expansion programme by buying new printing machines. Demand is very high and stocks have been very low. The managers plan to build up stocks, especially before the end of the year when most calendars are sold. The finance director allows retail customers a long time to pay Zippo's for supplies. She said 'By giving shops more credit we can gain extra orders'. The finance director is constructing a cash flow forecast for the next three months. She sees real problems arising for the business. The three month cash flow forecast is shown below:

Table 1: Zippo Printers Ltd three month cash flow forecast ($)

Cash in:	October	November	December
Cash from sales	8,000	12,000	15,000
Loans received	14,000	–	–
Total cash in:	22,000	12,000	15,000
Cash out:			
Materials	3,000	4,000	6,000
Labour	4,500	5,000	5,500
Overheads	1,000	1,000	1,000
Purchase of fixed assets	8,000	6,000	8,000
Total cash out:	X	16,000	20,500
Opening balance	3,000	8,500	Z
Net cash flow	5,500	Y	(5,500)
Closing balance	8,500	4,500	(1,000)

a) Calculate the figures missing as shown above as X, Y and Z.

[6 marks]

Marks *2 marks for each correct answer – 1 mark for good attempt at calculation.*

Student's answer The total cash out in October = $3,000 + $4,500 + $1,000 + $8,000 = $16,500. So X should be $16,500.
Net cash flow = cash in – cash out. In November this = $12,000 – $16,000 = $4,000 so Y = $4,000.
The opening balance in December will be the same as the closing balance in November, so Z = $4,500.

Examiner's marks and comments *X is correct so 2 marks. 1 mark for Y because although the number is correct, the net cash flow is negative and should be shown as ($4000). Z is correct so 2 marks. Total = 5/6 marks.*

b) Explain one benefit to Zippo's finance director of this cash flow forecast.

[4 marks]

Marks *1 mark for identifying a benefit; 1 mark for applying to Zippo's forecast and 2 marks for explaining why it is a benefit.*

Student's answer The cash flow forecast helps firms plan for future loans. It looks as though Zippo's will need a loan in December as the cash flow forecast is negative. By producing this forecast, a bank is more likely to offer a loan as it shows that the company is planning carefully.

Examiner's marks and comments *This is correct. The student has explained one use of cash flow forecasts well, and taken information from Zippo's forecast. 4 marks.*

c) What could be done to improve the cash flow of this business? Identify *two* ways of improving Zippo's cash flow from the list below. [2 marks]
- Reducing sales
- Increasing material purchases
- Paying suppliers more slowly
- Obtaining a loan
- Offering less credit to retail shops

Marks *1 mark for each correct point identified.*

Student's answer Obtaining a loan, offering retail shops less credit.

Examiner's marks and comments *2 marks – both correct.*

d) Using the two ways you have identified, explain to Zippo's finance director the advantages and disadvantages of these two ways of improving cash flow. [6 marks]

Marks *2 marks for applying points to Zippo; 2 marks for explaining in detail and 2 marks for evaluation.*

Student's answer A loan will give the company more cash. It could ask the bank to pay this loan in December so that cash flow does not become negative. The firm will have to pay interest on the loan, which will add to the overheads of the business.

Offering less credit to retail shops will mean fewer debtors, thereby turning customer debts into cash and improving cash flow.

Examiner's marks and comments *Brief, but accurate. 3 marks for the first paragraph – all skills are shown. 2 marks for the second paragraph – there is no evaluation. The student could have said that shops may stop buying cards from Zippo's and buy cards from a firm that offers more credit. 5/6 marks.*

Common misconceptions and errors

Error	Why it is wrong
'New businesses do not need cash flow forecasts as they have only just started.'	They need cash flow forecasts more than most firms! They need them to: a) apply for start-up loans from banks b) encourage people to invest in the business c) manage cash flows at a very expensive time in a business's life cycle.

Error	Why it is wrong
Confusing cash flow with profit: 'If a firm is making a profit it will have a good cash flow.'	Cash and profit are very different. A profitable business can run out of cash. A loss-making business could have plenty of cash, for example, ACE Suit Co. Ltd in March 2005:
	Sales = 200 suits at $75 = $15,000 Variable costs = $25 per suit = $5,000 Fixed costs = $3,000 Profit in March = $7,000
	BUT if half of the suits were sold on credit and all costs were paid in cash:
	Cash in = $7,500 Cash out = $8,000 Net cash flow = ($500)
Forgetting the negative signs – put figures in brackets.	Mistakes will be made with minus additions if the minus signs are not shown.

● **Try this**   Rishav and Abdullah are friends who want to set up their own radio station. They will need a large amount of equipment. The finance will come from investors and the bank and they also plan to sell advertising space. It will take several weeks for firms to pay for advertisements so the friends will have to attract many listeners first. Their accountant has constructed a cash flow forecast for the first three months:

($)

	May	June	July
Cash in from advertisements	0	1,500	3,000
Capital and loans	4,000		
Cash out:			
Purchase of equipment	5,000	2,000	0
Salaries	500	500	500
Overheads	1,000	1,000	1,000
Total cash out:	6,500	3,500	1,500
Opening balance	0	(2,500)	(4,500)
Net cash flow	(2,500)	X	1,500
Closing balance	(2,500)	(4,500)	(3,000)

a) Calculate the value of net cash flow in June.   [1 mark]

b) What is meant by the term 'closing balance'?   [2 marks]

c) Use the cash flow forecast and the case to explain why the closing balance is negative at the end of July.   [4 marks]

d) Explain why it was so important to Rishav and Abdullah to have this cash flow forecast before they started their business.   [6 marks]

Examiner's tip
✓ *Explain how a cash flow forecast helps with planning the finance needs of a new business – use the figures in the table to help you.*

UNIT 9 Financing business activity

Key objectives
- To understand why businesses need finance
- To explain the advantages and disadvantages of different sources of finance
- To understand which sources of finance are most suitable in different situations

Key definitions

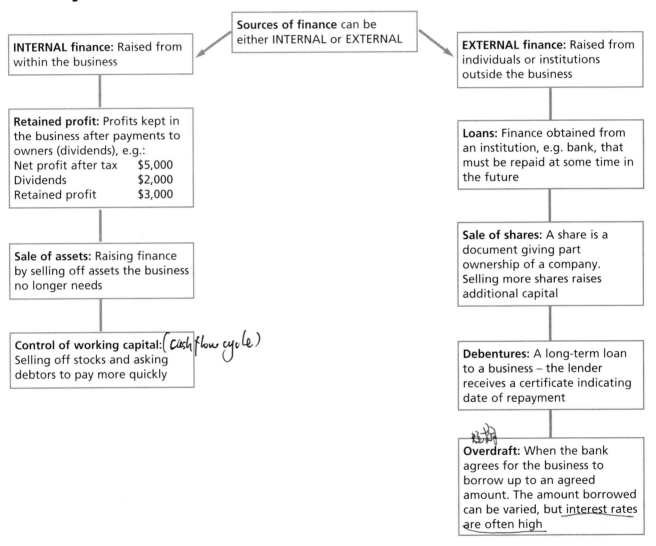

Sources of finance can be either INTERNAL or EXTERNAL

INTERNAL finance: Raised from within the business

Retained profit: Profits kept in the business after payments to owners (dividends), e.g.:
Net profit after tax $5,000
Dividends $2,000
Retained profit $3,000

Sale of assets: Raising finance by selling off assets the business no longer needs

Control of working capital: (Cash flow cycle)
Selling off stocks and asking debtors to pay more quickly

EXTERNAL finance: Raised from individuals or institutions outside the business

Loans: Finance obtained from an institution, e.g. bank, that must be repaid at some time in the future

Sale of shares: A share is a document giving part ownership of a company. Selling more shares raises additional capital

Debentures: A long-term loan to a business – the lender receives a certificate indicating date of repayment

Overdraft: When the bank agrees for the business to borrow up to an agreed amount. The amount borrowed can be varied, but interest rates are often high

Term	Definition	Examples
Debt factoring	This is the sale of debt invoices (money owed to a business by its customers) to a specialist finance organisation.	If a customer owes a business $60,000 to be paid in three months' time, the business could sell this invoice to a debt factor for immediate cash, but at a discount.
Leasing	Obtaining the use of an asset in exchange for regular leasing charges instead of buying it outright.	Many computers are leased to businesses – they become outdated quickly, so purchasing them can be a disadvantage.
Hire purchase	This allows a business to purchase an asset by making monthly payments over a period of time.	This is an alternative to using cash to buy the asset outright.
Trade credit *to sales revenue to pay the raw materials.*	Credit gained from suppliers.	A supplier delivers goods valued at $2,000, but these will be paid for in two months' time.
Business plan	A report that gives details of the marketing, production and financial plans of a new business start-up.	See page 139 in IGCSE textbook (2nd edition).
Start-up finance (capital) *Should be enough to run the business*	The capital needed to set up a new business.	Finance will be needed for such assets as buildings and stocks before trading can begin.
Capital expenditure	Spending on fixed assets that will last more than one year.	Buildings, machinery and vehicles
Revenue expenditure	Spending on day-to-day expenses, not fixed assets.	Wages, purchase of materials and electricity

Sample questions and answers

Sample questions 1) Heathwood Engineering plc needs additional finance. The business has three spending plans. Select *one* source of finance from the list below for each plan. State *one* reason for the source of finance selected in each case.

Spending plan	Suitable source of finance	Reason for choice
New computers for the office		
Takeover of a rival business		
Temporary increase in stocks		

Sources of finance: Issue of shares
Leasing
Trade credit
Long-term loan [6 marks]

Marks *1 mark for each appropriate source plus 1 mark for relevant reason.*

Student's answer

Spending plan	Suitable source of finance	Reason for choice
New computers for the office	Leasing	As computers will become out of date quickly, Heathwood does not actually want to own them.
Takeover of a rival business	Issue of shares	The takeover is likely to be expensive and issues of shares can raise a lot of capital. A long-term loan will lead to high interest payments.
Temporary increase in stocks	Trade credit	No need for a long-term loan if the increase in stocks is temporary.

Examiner's marks and comments *Full marks – correct choices and good reasons given.*

2) Jill and Zuki are two friends who want to open a new beauty salon. They are both skilled hairdressers, but they have not owned their own business before. They are applying for a large bank loan to help with 'set-up' costs.

    i) What 'set-up' costs will need to be paid before the business starts to trade? State *two* examples. [2 marks]

Marks *1 mark each for appropriate costs identified.*

Student's answer Rent of premises, purchase of hairdryers.

Examiner's marks and comments *2 marks.*

    ii) State *three* questions that the bank manager is likely to ask Jill and Zuki before giving the loan. Briefly explain why each question is important. [6 marks]

Marks *1 mark for each relevant question; 1 mark for each relevant reason.*

Student's answer Q1. Where are you setting up your business?
Reason: So that he can tell whether it is a good area for this type of business.

Q2. Have you done any market research?
Reason: So that he can tell whether the two friends have looked into the possible demand.

Q3. How much money are Jill and Zuki going to invest?
Reason: So that the bank manager can see that the bank will not be taking all of the risk.

Examiner's marks and comments *Full marks again – three good questions plus relevant reasons.*

3) i) What do you understand by a business plan? [2 marks]

Marks *2 marks for good understanding; 1 mark for some understanding.*

Student's answer A business plan contains details of a new business start-up including market research and aims of the business.

Examiner's marks and comments

There is enough understanding shown for 2 marks.

ii) Jill and Zuki decide to draw up a business plan. Will this convince the bank manager to give a loan? Explain your answer. [6 marks]

Marks

2 marks for explaining what a business plan would contain for this business (knowledge and application); 2 marks for analysing how it could influence the decision; 2 marks for evaluating its impact on the decision.

Student's answer

In their business plan, Jill and Zuki will present useful information about their idea for the beauty salon. They should include market research about other salons, details of their experience, where the salon will be located and how much finance they will need. This will definitely mean that the bank manager will lend them all the money they need. The manager will see that they have thought about the business and so will be prepared to lend the money.

Try to mark this yourself – examiner's marks and comments are on page 102.

Common misconceptions and errors

Error	Why it is wrong
'All limited companies can sell more shares on the Stock Exchange.'	Only public limited companies can do this – private limited companies cannot do this.
'Selling more shares is an example of internal finance.'	Even though shareholders own a company they are 'outside' providers of capital – the company is a separate legal unit. Sale of shares is external finance.
'Shares are a form of long-term loan.'	No – shares do not have to be repaid by the company. All loans have to be repaid eventually.
'An overdraft is a long-term loan.'	No – an overdraft can be called back by a bank at short notice. A long-term loan is for an agreed period, usually more than ten years.

● Try this

a) The table below lists three sources of business finance. Copy the table and briefly explain *one* advantage and *one* disadvantage of each source.

[6 marks]

Source of finance	Advantage	Disadvantage
Issue of new shares by a company		
Overdraft		
Long-term loan		

b) Use the following table to indicate with a tick whether the following sources of finance are internal or external: [4 marks]

Source of finance	Internal	External
Debenture		
Issue of shares		
Retained profit		
Sale of buildings		

c) The directors of a public limited company are planning to double the size of the existing factory. This will cost $5m. The company already has substantial long-term loans. The directors still control just over 50% of the shares between them. They are considering four possible sources of finance: new share issue, long-term loan, overdraft, retained profits.

Advise the directors on the most suitable method of financing this expansion. Give reasons for your answer.   [8 marks]

Examiner's tip
✓ *Think about how long they will need the finance for.*

UNIT 10 Organisational structure

Key objectives

- To explain what is meant by 'organisational structure' and why businesses need one
- To understand how organisational structure can be shown on a diagram and why it changes as firms expand
- To analyse the different ideas connected to organisational structure
- To understand the impact of decentralisation on a business

Key definitions

The diagram below shows the typical organisational structure of a business. This structure shows how the business is organised internally with levels of responsibility:

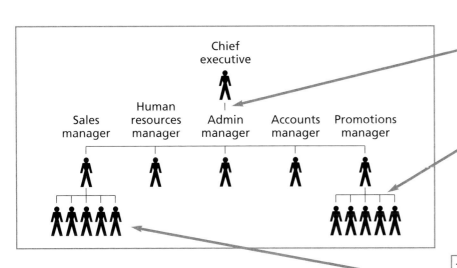

The vertical lines show the **chain of command** – the links through which instructions are passed down from managers to subordinates

The horizontal lines show the **levels of hierarchy** – the managers on each level have equal authority

The **span of control** is the number of staff who report to each manager. The span of control of the sales manager is five

Term	Definition	Examples
Delegation	Giving a subordinate the authority to do certain tasks.	A marketing manager may delegate the task of gathering market data to a worker in his or her department.
Hierarchy	The different levels of authority in the organisation.	The chart above shows the hierarchy of the business.
Tall structure	This type of organisation has many levels of hierarchy and small spans of control.	
Functional departments	Departments in an organisation that have responsibility for one part of the business.	Marketing Accounting Production
Line managers	Have direct responsibility for decisions and for the work of staff.	Marketing manager, accounts manager.
Staff manager	Specialist advisers who support the line managers and directors.	IT specialist, economist.

Term	Definition	Examples
Decentralisation	Taking decisions away from the centre of an organisation – away from Head Office.	The Egyptian division of the German car firm Mercedes may take many decisions without referring back to directors in Germany.

Sample questions and answers

Sample question Yuan's business has grown rapidly in three years. Setting her flower business up as a sole trader, Yuan had made all of the important decisions. Now she has three flower shops and a home delivery service. She employs an accountant, managers for the shops, and a transport manager. The current organisational structure is shown below:

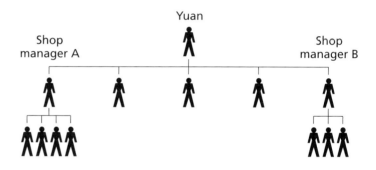

a) What is the span of control of shop manager A? [1 mark]

Marks *1 mark for correct answer of four.*

Student's answer Four people report to this manager.

Examiner's marks and comments *Good! 1 mark.*

b) How many levels of hierarchy are there in this business? [1 mark]

Marks *1 mark for correct answer of three.*

Student's answer There are four levels of hierarchy.

Examiner's marks and comments *No – there are only three levels including Yuan herself. 0 marks.*

c) If shop A expands and four more staff are employed, the manager's span of control will increase.
  i) Explain *one* advantage of this. [3 marks]
  ii) Explain *one* disadvantage of this. [3 marks]

Marks *1 mark for identifying each factor and up to 2 marks for explaining each one.*

Student's answer **i)** A wider span of control will mean that the manager will have to delegate more authority to each worker. This could mean that their jobs become more interesting.

Examiner's marks and comments *Full marks for an accurate and well explained answer.*

Student's answer **ii)** A wider span of control means a longer chain of command, so messages will take longer to reach the staff.

Examiner's marks and comments *No marks here – a wider span of control does not create more levels of hierarchy and therefore does not make the chain of command longer. The student could have explained the reduced control that the manager will have with a wider span of control.*

d) How do you think the organisational structure of Yuan's business might change if it continues to grow? Explain your answer.   [8 marks]

Marks *2 marks for identifying possible changes; 2 marks for applying them to this business; 2 marks for explaining/analysing changes and 2 marks for evaluation.*

Student's answer If Yuan's business grows, it will need a new structure. More departments will be needed, for example, marketing and human resources. Yuan might need to recruit some more senior managers, as she will not be able to take all of the decisions herself. A marketing director would help her to advertise the flower shops. The chain of command will get longer so that staff in the shops will have to wait longer for messages from the top. The structure will depend on the span of control that Yuan wants and whether she decides to decentralise the business. If she decides to grow flowers as well as sell them, a new division will be needed.

Try to mark this for yourself. The examiner's marks and comments are on page 103.

Common misconceptions and errors

Error	Why it is wrong
'Delegation is giving all responsibility to workers.'	Delegation gives authority or power to workers to do a job – the manager still has the final responsibility.
'Staff managers control the staff.'	Staff manages are specialist advisers – they do not control the line workers in the business.
'A wider span of control means that more managers are needed.'	A wider span of control means that more workers report to each manager – so *fewer* managers might be needed.

● **Try this** Ahmed Clothing Ltd is a clothing manufacturer. It has three factories in three different countries. Each factory is controlled by a factory manager who is helped by three production supervisors. Each supervisor controls the work of five production line workers.

a) Sketch the organisation chart for *one* of Ahmed's factories.   [4 marks]

b) The company has three levels of management at Head Office. The business is controlled by Abadullah Ahmed. He believes in taking all of the important decisions himself. The factory managers have to ensure that Abadullah's designs of clothes are followed. Each factory pays its workers exactly the same wages. Methods of production are decided on by Abadullah and his Head Office managers.

i) Explain *one* problem that could result from having many levels of hierarchy. [4 marks]

ii) Would you describe Ahmed Clothing Ltd as being a centralised business? Explain your answer. [4 marks]

iii) Discuss whether Abadullah should decentralise his business. [8 marks]

Examiner's tip
✓ *You should try to define decentralisation, give advantages and disadvantages and then make a decision.*

UNIT 11 Managing a business

Key objectives
- To explain the role of managers in business
- To understand the qualities needed for a good manager
- To outline the different management responsibilities within different departments

Key definitions

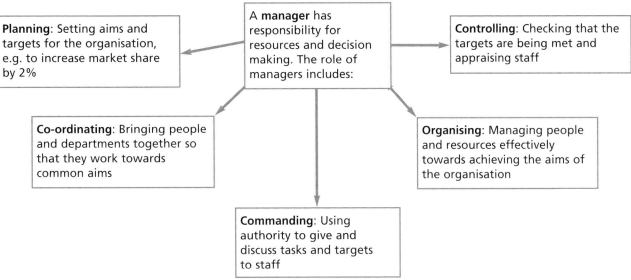

Planning: Setting aims and targets for the organisation, e.g. to increase market share by 2%

A **manager** has responsibility for resources and decision making. The role of managers includes:

Controlling: Checking that the targets are being met and appraising staff

Co-ordinating: Bringing people and departments together so that they work towards common aims

Organising: Managing people and resources effectively towards achieving the aims of the organisation

Commanding: Using authority to give and discuss tasks and targets to staff

Term	Definition	Examples
Initiative	Ability to work on one's own and to make suggestions for solving problems.	If quality of output is falling, a manager might come up with an idea to improve it.
Strategic decisions	Important, long-term decisions, that can affect the overall success of the business.	Pepsi decides to open their own cafés.
Tactical decisions	Frequently taken and less important decisions.	Should we buy trucks or lease them?
Operational decisions	Day-to-day decisions taken within each department.	Which dresses should we put in the shop window?
Decision-making process	The stages a manager should go through before taking an important decision – shown by the decision-making flow chart:	See figure below.

1 Objectives of the business → 2 Identify the problem → 3 Collect and analyse data → 4 Consider options and take decision → 5 Review – was it successful? → (back to 1 Objectives of the business)

Term	Definition	Examples
Chief Executive (Managing Director)	The director (or senior manager) in charge of all operations within a business.	Try to find out the name of the Chief Executive of a well known company in your country.

Term	Definition	Examples
Human resources manager	Responsible for all aspects of training, motivating and appraising staff.	The manager will negotiate with trade unions on pay. The manager will prepare job descriptions and job specifications for recruiting new staff.
Marketing manager	Responsible for all aspects of market research, the marketing mix, and sales performance of products.	The manager will decide the price at which each product is sold. If this is too high, few consumers will buy it.
Finance and accounts manager	Responsible for keeping financial records, producing annual accounts, and controlling cash flows.	If the net cash flow is negative, this manager will be responsible for raising additional finance.
Operations manager (Production manager)	Responsible for producing the product/service in the right quantities and to the correct quality level.	Ordering stocks of raw materials, checking on quality standards, using the most appropriate production methods.
Administration manager	Responsible for clerical work, IT equipment, and maintenance of buildings.	Keeping records and official documents, maintaining the computer system and arranging maintenance to the buildings when necessary.

Sample questions and answers

Sample questions 1) Match the areas of responsibility (see list below) to the manager: [4 marks]

Manager	Responsible for:
Marketing	
Operations (Production)	
Finance	
Administration	

Areas of responsibility:

i) arranging bank loans
ii) deciding which newspaper to advertise in
iii) checking on quality levels
iv) organising the post room for despatch of letters.

Marks *1 mark for each correct answer.*

Student's answer

Manager	Responsible for:
Marketing	Deciding which newspaper to advertise in
Operations (Production)	Checking on quality levels
Finance	Arranging bank loans
Administration	Organising the post room for despatch of letters

Examiner's marks and comments *4 marks – all correct.*

2) Harry owns a TV repair shop. He employs five mechanics and two administration staff. He plans to open a new branch in another town. He needs to recruit a manager for this shop. The manager will have to organise the workers, and deal with customers and all problems. Explain *two* qualities that you think a successful manager of Harry's new shop is likely to have.

[6 marks]

Marks *1 mark for each point and 1 mark for putting each point into context; 1 further mark for explaining each point.*

Student's answer The manager will need to be knowledgeable about television repair. It will be easier for the manager to run the shop if he or she, as well as the workers, has the ability to repair the televisions. The manager will also need good communication skills so that he or she can speak clearly.

Examiner's marks and comments *4/6 marks. Two relevant points were made, but only the first was developed in the context of TV repairs. The second point, about good communication skills, could have been developed by explaining that these would be necessary to make technical details clear to customers.*

Common misconceptions and errors

Error	Why it is wrong
'Managers just give orders to other workers.'	There are so many other parts of a manager's job – and would 'giving orders' be a very effective style of management?
'If managers take decisions carefully, there will be no risks for the business.'	Even the best managers taking the best decisions will have to accept some risk – changes to the economy, for example, are not under the control of managers.
'Human resources managers just recruit and sack staff.'	HR managers also have responsibility for training, staff appraisal, negotiating with unions, keeping staff records and motivating staff.

● **Try this** **a)** Explain *one* reason why you think it is important for a manager to set aims or targets for the business. [4 marks]

b) A manager is worried about falling profits. She knows that a major change is needed to solve this problem. Before taking a decision she

47 ●

decides to use the decision-making flow chart. Fill in the gaps using the sentences below:

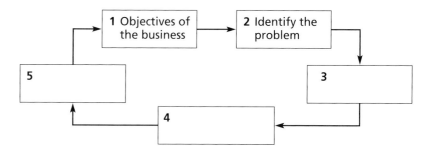

Collect and analyse data

Review – was it successful?

Consider options and take decision [3 marks]

c) Umeel is retiring after 25 years of managing his own restaurant. It is a very successful business. He employs 25 trained staff and needs to recruit a new manager. After advertising the job, he must decide between two applicants. He has gathered the following information about them:

Details	Person A	Person B
Age	35	55
Education	Business degree	A levels
Restaurant experience	3 years as junior manager.	20 years as chef and then 5 years as manager.
Main business skills	Motivating staff, good communicator.	Cooking, ordering right amount of stocks.
'Describe your main personal qualities'	'I am a natural leader and I am ambitious for myself and the restaurant.'	'I am a very hard worker. I enjoy giving people pleasure with the food I cook.'
'What plans would you have for the restaurant?'	'I would aim to double its size and employ more staff.'	'I would like to encourage staff to cook even higher quality food.'

On the basis of this information, which person would you choose for the manager's job? Justify your answer. [10 marks]

Examiner's tip

✓ *Think of the qualities of a good manager and apply these to the information above. The final choice might depend on the aims that Umeel has for the business.*

UNIT 12 Communication in business

Key objectives

- To understand why good communication is important to business
- To explain the advantages and disadvantages of different communication methods
- To examine why barriers to communication exist and how they can be reduced

Key definitions

The **sender** of the message should send it in clear language and using the most appropriate method

One–way communication allows for no **feedback**, e.g. a safety notice on a fire door

The **communication method** or **medium** is how the message is sent, for example, written e-mail or a face-to-face conversation

Feedback allows for two-way communication, e.g. a reply to a question

The **receiver** should understand and act upon the message. If asked for, **feedback** should be given

Term	Definition	Examples
Verbal or spoken communication	The sender speaks directly to the receiver(s).	1. Telephone 2. Meetings 3. Conversation
Written communication	The message is sent in a written form.	1. Letters 2. Memos 3. E-mails
Visual communication	The message is put into a form that can be understood visually, not written or spoken.	1. Graph of sales figures 2. Video 3. Posters
Formal communication	Messages sent by using the channels set up by the organisation.	1. Reports 2. Minutes from a meeting
Informal communication	Messages through the 'grapevine' of informal contacts.	Staff talking at breaks or lunchtimes.
Barriers to communication	The reasons why communication fails.	1. Unclear language 2. Too many levels of hierarchy 3. Using the wrong method
Internal communication	Messages sent and received by people within the organisation.	1. Manager talking to workers 2. Notice on company notice board or intranet
External communication	Messages sent outside of the organisation.	1. An order sent to a supplier 2. Letter to a customer

Sample questions and answers

Sample questions

1) Choose the best method of communication. Match the *message* (table A) with the *method of communication* (table B). [4 marks]

A – the message	B – the method of communication
a) List of staff names who have First Aid training	**i)** Letter
b) Urgent order to supplier	**ii)** Telephone call
c) Detailed map of how to get to the factory to be sent to ten visitors arriving this afternoon	**iii)** Notice board
d) Contract of employment for new worker	**iv)** E-mail

Marks

1 mark for each correct answer.

Student's answer

a) = iii)

b) = ii)

c) = iv)

d) = i)

Examiner's marks and comments

Full marks – do you understand why these are the correct methods to use?

2) Explain *two* advantages of managers using meetings with staff as a main form of communication. [4 marks]

Marks

1 mark each for identifying an advantage plus 1 mark each for explaining.

Student's answer

Meetings between a manager and workers allow for feedback. This means that if the worker does not understand the message then he or she can ask for more information.

Another advantage is that workers might be more motivated.

Examiner's marks and comments

3 marks awarded, 2 for two benefits, but only one of them is explained. The student could have added that by allowing talking and discussion between manager and staff, the worker will feel more involved and keen to work hard.

Common misconceptions and errors

Error	Why it is wrong
'Communication is always more effective via computer.'	It *may* be true that computers aid communication, for example, internet and e-mails, but it is not *always* the case. They can break down and often lead to too many messages being sent – the receiver may not be able to tell which are the most important ones.
'Two-way communication is a waste of time.'	Two-way communication *may* take more time than one-way, but it has many benefits. It allows for feedback, questions and involvement of the staff.

Error	Why it is wrong
'Letters are the best form of communication.'	This is often not true. They can be too formal and time consuming – they also do not allow for immediate feedback. The choice of the best medium of communication must take many factors into account.

● **Try this**   A marketing manager for a sweet manufacturer wants to send a message to the owners of the 25 retail shops that sell the firm's product. The message gives details about an exciting new product with colourful packaging and a new brand name.

a) Is this an example of internal or external communication? Explain your answer briefly.   [2 marks]

b) Would you advise the manager to use a telephone call to every shop owner, an e-mail message to each shop, or a video sent to all shop owners plus posters? Justify the method of communication you choose.   [8 marks]

c) 'As my business has expanded to over 400 workers, I find it more and more difficult to communicate with staff. They just do not read my notices. I think I will send them a newsletter each week,' the managing director of a large suit-making company told his secretary. Explain *two* possible barriers to communication resulting from using either **notices on boards** or **newsletters**.   [6 marks]

UNIT 13 Motivation at work

Key objectives

- To understand the different motivation theories
- To understand what motivates workers
- To know about the different types of payment methods and other ways workers can be motivated
- To understand how to choose suitable ways of giving job satisfaction to different types of work
- To understand different styles of leadership

Key definitions

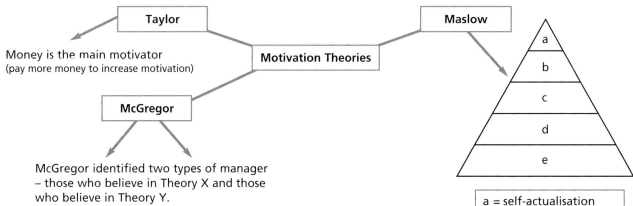

Taylor

Money is the main motivator
(pay more money to increase motivation)

Motivation Theories

Maslow

a	
b	
c	
d	
e	

McGregor

McGregor identified two types of manager – those who believe in Theory X and those who believe in Theory Y.

Theory X
The average person does not like work. Workers must be constantly supervised so they will work. Motivation is from external factors, e.g. pay schemes where the workers are paid more for increased output

Theory Y
The average person is motivated by internal factors. To motivate workers, you need to find ways to help workers take an interest in their work, e.g. give rewards/incentives

a = self-actualisation
b = esteem needs
c = social needs
d = safety/security needs
e = physiological needs

Progress up the hierarchy (from e to a) – satisfy/achieve one level, then can move to the next level. Don't necessarily have to pay more but can find different ways to motivate workers as they move up the levels

Term	Description	Examples
Motivation	Reason why workers want to work hard and work effectively for the business.	Motivation can be increased by: (a) monetary rewards (b) non-monetary rewards (c) introducing ways to give job satisfaction.
(a) Monetary rewards	**Wage:** payment for work, usually paid weekly. Can be calculated by the number of hours worked (called **time rate**) and paid overtime or can be paid depending on the quantity of products made (called **piece rate**).	$10 per hour plus overtime $10 per product produced

Term	Description	Examples
	Salary: payment for work, usually paid monthly. In addition, some salaried workers also get **commission** paid (more pay the more goods they sell) or **profit sharing** (share of the profits paid to employees) or **bonus** (lump sum paid to workers if they have worked well) or **performance-related pay** (pay which is related to the effectiveness of the employee).	$10,000 per year
(b) Non-monetary rewards	Sometimes called **fringe benefits**. These are extra benefits given to employees in addition to their pay.	Children's education fees paid, discounts on the firm's products, health care fees paid, free accommodation, company car.
(c) Job satisfaction	The enjoyment a worker gets from feeling that they have done a good job. There are three main ways to motivate workers to be more committed to their job and work more effectively:	
	Job rotation (swapping workers round and only doing a specific task for a limited time before swapping round again).	Packing for an hour, filling containers for an hour, labelling for an hour, etc.
	Job enlargement (extra tasks are added to the job to make it more interesting – they should be at a similar skill level).	Warehouse worker unpacks goods, sorts orders, stacks shelves, picks orders, etc.
	Job enrichment (adding tasks that require more skill and/or responsibility).	Hotel receptionist answers the telephone, deals with enquiries, takes bookings, word processes letters, etc.
Leadership styles	Good management and leadership style are important for motivation. A good leader is someone who can inspire and get the best out of the workers. There are three main types of leadership style: **autocratic, laissez–faire, democratic.**	Autocratic leadership (manager in charge and gives orders). Laissez–faire leadership (manager gives broad objectives and leaves the workers to organise their own way of achieving these objectives). Democratic leadership (manager gets workers involved in the decision making).

Sample questions and answers

Sample questions **1)** Why might improved motivation of employees increase productivity? [4 marks]

Marks *1 mark for knowledge that if motivation is high then the desire to achieve goals is higher; 3 marks if there is a clear linkage between increased motivation and the increase in performance.*

Student's answer As more workers are motivated then they will all be happy to come to work every day, thus reducing absenteeism. If people are more motivated, they will work harder for the business to their best ability to try to produce as many goods or services as possible. Also, if there are promotion opportunities, they will try to impress the manager and as a result production will increase.

53 ●

Examiner's marks and comments — *A good answer with several reasons given as to why productivity might increase. Full marks.*

2) Explain one method that a business could use, which might increase the motivation of its workforce. [3 marks]

Marks — *1 mark for the method; 2 marks for explaining the impact on motivation.*

Student's answer — Job satisfaction – the workforce needs to be satisfied with their jobs by having better working conditions, knowing there are chances of promotion, and good wages. Job rotation helps to improve job satisfaction – a group of employees divide themselves and take shifts at certain times.

Examiner's marks and comments — *Only one method can be rewarded, so 1 mark. The other methods were not needed and none of the methods was explained.*

3) The graph shows the weekly wages paid to production workers at Mimmus plc.

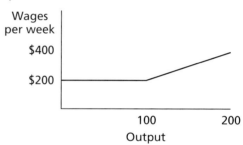

i) Mimmus plc pays its workers using the payment method shown in the graph above. What method of payment is it using? Explain your answer. [3 marks]

Marks — *1 mark for identifying a set amount of wages paid up to an output of 100 units; 2 marks for explaining that the piece rate is then used: that is, the more output produced above 100 units, the more wages are paid.*

Student's answer — The workers are paid $200 per week no matter how much they produce. After that, piece rate is paid.

Try to mark this yourself – the examiner's marks and comment are on page 104.

ii) Calculate how much the worker will earn if he or she produces 150 units of output. [2 marks]

Marks — *Correct answer 2 marks; 1 mark if correct method, but incorrect answer.*

Student's answer — $200 + (50 × $2) = $300

Try to mark this yourself – the examiner's marks and comments are on page 104.

Common misconceptions and errors

Error	Why it is wrong
'Increasing pay will always motivate workers to work harder.'	Increasing pay can improve motivation, but it will not work every time and businesses may need to find other ways to motivate workers.

Error	Why it is wrong
'Time rate is paid at a set period of time, for example, each week.'	Time rate is the amount paid per hour worked and may be paid weekly, but so may piece rate.
'Piece rate is where workers get a set amount of pay and then are paid more if they produce more.'	Piece rate refers to wages being related to the output produced and does not refer to a set amount paid whether the worker produces more or not.
'Job enlargement is when more tasks are added to someone's job description and they need extra training to do the extra more difficult tasks.'	Job enlargement involves additional tasks being added to the job but they should be of a similar skill level. If they are more difficult tasks then this is job enrichment.

● **Try this**   Patel Fashions is a retail business which sells women's clothes. It employs 15 sales staff who work in the shop and five more who work in the offices. There is one shop manager who is in charge of the business. Each of the sales staff has a specific job and they only do this one task. For example, some just serve customers at the pay desk, some look after the fitting room, and others look after the clothes on display. Employees keep leaving and the shop manager regularly has to advertise for new employees. 'I do not like having to spend so much time interviewing applicants for sales assistant jobs. I wish the employees would not keep leaving,' said Marie, the shop manager.

a) Discuss the different financial and non-financial benefits the store manager could use to improve motivation at the shop, In order to prevent workers from leaving so regularly. Which would be the best method for her to employ and why? [12 marks]

> **Examiner's tip**
> ✓ *Explain the advantages and disadvantages of different financial and non-financial methods of motivation. Select one method and explain why you think it is the best one for Patel Fashions to use.*

b) Would job rotation be the best method for Marie to use in order to increase job satisfaction? Explain your answer. [8 marks]

> **Examiner's tip**
> ✓ *Explain how Patel Fashions could use job rotation, job enlargement and job enrichment. Say whether you consider job rotation to be the best method and why.*

c) State which management style (democratic/autocratic/laissez-faire) you would suggest for **i)** Theory X managers and **ii)** Theory Y managers. Explain your choice. [6 marks]

UNIT 14 Recruitment, training and human resources

Key objectives

- To understand the role of the human resources department
- To understand the recruitment and selection process
- To appreciate the different types of training
- To know the difference between redundancy and dismissal

Key definitions

The recruitment and selection process

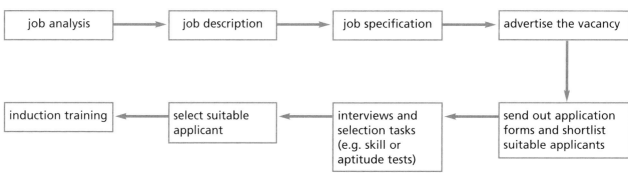

Term	Description	Examples
Job analysis	Identification of the tasks and responsibilities to be carried out by the person doing the job.	A receptionist leaves a company and when Human Resources looks at the job description, it is realised that some of the tasks are no longer needed. However, the business does need someone with more IT skills. The receptionist's job description therefore needs to be rewritten.
Job description	The tasks, duties and responsibilities someone will need to carry out as part of a specific job.	The receptionist's job description now includes processing orders onto the computer. The receptionist is not required to answer as many queries because a new telephone system now does this.
Job (person) specification	The required qualifications, skills, personal qualities, etc. for a specific job.	The receptionist's job specification will need to include IT skills in addition to the usual qualifications and skills of a receptionist.
Internal recruitment	Vacancy is filled by a person who is an existing employee.	Shop assistant is promoted to supervisor. The job is advertised on the company notice board or a large business may have a company newspaper or intranet.
External recruitment	Vacancy is filled by a person who is not an existing employee and will be new to the business.	A new store manager has been appointed who currently works for another shop. The job was advertised in local newspapers, national newspapers, specialist magazines and journals, recruitment agencies or centres run by the government (job centres).

Term	Description	Examples
Induction training	An introduction to the business for a new employee.	New employee is shown round the business, introduced to other workers, given Health & Safety instructions, given information on rules and regulations of the business.
On-the-job training	Training is given at the place of work by watching another, more experienced employee doing the job.	A production line worker is shown what to do by another experienced production line worker.
Off-the-job training	Training is given away from the place of work itself. Can be at a different place such as a college or could be at the business's site, but in a different building.	In a classroom using lecture, role play, case studies, or computer simulations.
Redundancy/retrenchment	The shedding of employees because the business changes.	The business introduces new technology or closes a factory, therefore fewer workers are needed.
Dismissal	The employee is no longer employed because he or she is unsatisfactory in some way.	An employee is sacked because he or she is caught stealing stock.

Sample questions and answers

Sample questions

1) Why do businesses carry out a job analysis when an employee leaves? [4 marks]

Marks *2 marks for giving reasons for a job analysis to be drawn up; 2 marks for explaining why these reasons are important to the business.*

Student's answer A business carries out a job analysis to see whether it needs to replace the worker with someone who can do exactly the same job. After that, it will draw up a job description outlining all tasks and duties that the job involves and then a job specification, which states the skills and qualifications that the applicants must have.

Examiner's marks and comments *The first sentence attempts to answer the question, but the rest of the response does not directly answer it. The candidate needs to discuss in more detail why a job analysis is carried out and an example would have helped to explain the answer. Drawing up a job description would then follow, but only when it has been decided exactly what the job must involve after the job analysis is complete. 1 mark.*

2) CDF Ltd has just introduced new technology into the business. It finds that its employees do not have the appropriate skills needed to operate this new equipment.

i) Why might this be a problem for CDF Ltd? [4 marks]

Marks *2 marks for problems stated; 2 marks for explaining the problems.*

Student's answer If the workers do not have the correct skills then training will be needed. The costs of training and/or recruiting new staff can be very high. In addition, while the training takes place, the output of CDF Ltd is likely to decrease because the workers are either co-operating with trainers or are the trainers themselves. Also, if employees cannot operate the new technology they might fear that they will lose their job and therefore morale may be low.

Examiner's marks and comments

A good answer – full marks. Three problems are stated and then explained as to why they are a problem for the business. Only two problems were needed for full marks.

ii) How would you suggest that CDF Ltd deals with this problem? [6 marks]

Marks

3 marks for limited suggestions not really explained; 3 further marks if suggestions are explained.

Student's answer

I suggest that it trains some of its employees straight away to operate the new technology so that they do not spend time once the machinery has arrived. It could also advertise for new employees who are already trained, but this would mean that some of the current workers would need to be sacked.

Try to mark this yourself – the examiner's marks and comments are on page 105.

Common misconceptions and errors

Error	Why it is wrong
'A job description states the qualifications needed for a particular job.'	The job description outlines the duties that are involved in the job. A job specification outlines the qualifications and skills that are needed to carry out the job.
'On-the-job training does not cost anything because an existing employee trains the new employee.'	On-the-job training does cost money because the experienced employee cannot work at the usual rate while showing the trainee what to do. The employee will also need to keep watching the trainee to make sure he or she is doing the job properly. This means the company is paying the experienced worker, but he or she is not producing the usual quantity of goods.
'On-the-job training is suitable for a skilled worker, for example, an accountant.'	On-the-job training is only really suitable for unskilled or semi-skilled workers. An accountant would need to be trained at college for most of the time and not just at his or her place of work. There would be insufficient time whilst working to go over all the information required to become fully qualified.
'Off-the-job training is always away from the business's premises.'	Off-the-job training is away from the place of work itself, but can still be on the same site.

Try this

a) Suggest three reasons why employees might leave their job. [3 marks]

b) If a lot of employees left every year, why might this be a problem for the business? [6 marks]

> **Examiner's tip**
> ✓ Include why they are leaving, costs of replacing them, training, morale.

c) Why do businesses carry out induction training? [4 marks]

d) The Royal Garden is a hotel in the centre of a city. It employs many workers in the restaurant and the department which cleans and services rooms. Most of these workers have few skills. In the restaurant there are also trained employees who work in the kitchens preparing food.

i) The Royal Garden wants to increase the number of restaurants it has and therefore needs to employ more staff to work in the kitchens. Discuss whether it should use internal or external recruitment for the new chefs to work in the restaurants. [12 marks]

> **Examiner's tip**
> ✓ Explain the advantages and disadvantages of internal and external recruitment. Make a judgement as to which would be the better one to use and why.

ii) The Royal Garden has recruited several waiters and waitresses to work in the new restaurants. What type of training would you suggest the management use to train them? Justify your choice. [5 marks]

> **Examiner's tip**
> ✓ Choose a type of training, either on-the-job or off-the-job, and explain why it would be suitable to train these low-skilled employees.

UNIT 15 Employee and employer associations

Key objectives
- To recognise the different types of trade unions
- To understand how trade unions benefit employees and their role in businesses
- To understand the process of collective bargaining
- To know what happens when conflict arises and the different types of industrial action
- To understand the role of employer associations
- To know how conflict can be avoided or solved

Key definitions

Term	Description	Examples
Trade union	An organisation formed by a group of workers, which represents their interests. The reasons for joining together include strength in numbers, negotiating pay on behalf of its members, representing workers in grievances with management, advice if dismissed/made redundant, advice if unfairly treated, improved working conditions.	National Union of Teachers (NUT). National Union of Rail, Maritime and Transport Workers (RMT).
Craft union	Represents a particular type of skilled worker.	An electricians' union.
General union	Represents workers from a variety of trades and industries.	Skilled and unskilled workers in a union which represents workers in different industries.
Industrial union	Represents all types of workers in a particular industry.	A union which represents all workers in the mining industry.
White-collar union	Represents non-manual workers.	A union which represents office workers.
Employer associations	An organisation formed by a group of employers to give benefits to its members. The reasons for joining together include strength in being a large group, acts as a pressure group, represents the employers and negotiates with trade unions, shares ideas amongst the members, sometimes organises discounts for its members if buying in bulk.	Employers' Organisation for local government. Universities and Colleges Employers' Association.
Collective bargaining	Negotiations between the management of a business (or several businesses) and a trade union (or several trade unions) on pay and conditions of employment.	The management of a business negotiates pay rates with the trade union which represents the employees.

Term	Description	Examples
Industrial action	Action that may be taken by a trade union to put pressure on the management when in negotiations. It involves halting or decreasing production.	• Strike (employees refuse to work). • Picketing (employees who are taking industrial action stand outside their place of work to prevent or protest at goods or people going in and out of the business). • Work to rule (rules are strictly obeyed so that work is slowed down). • Go slow (employees do their normal work, but more slowly). • Non-co-operation (workers refuse to have anything to do with new working practices they disapprove of). • Overtime ban (refusal to do overtime).
Worker participation	Employees contribute to the decision-making process in the business.	Worker directors, works councils, quality circles, more democratic styles of leadership.

Sample questions and answers

Sample questions   1) Explain why workers join trade unions.   [6 marks]

Marks   *Up to 3 marks for stating the benefits of trade union membership; 3 marks for explaining why these are benefits to employees.*

Student's answer   If the worker joins a union then he or she will be part of a large group of employees, which has extra bargaining power when negotiating pay or conditions with the management. Pay should be better and if an employee is treated unfairly then the union will give him or her advice.

Examiner's marks and comments   *The first benefit is explained but the other two benefits are only stated and not explained. Therefore 4/6 marks were awarded.*

2) Toys Galore plc manufactures children's toys. The company produces dolls and dolls' clothes. The toys are sold all over the country and the business also exports 25% of its output. The workers want a wage increase, but the management has said that this is not possible.

   i)   Explain three types of industrial action that the union can advise the workers to take.   [6 marks]

Marks   *1 mark for each of the three types of industrial action; 1 mark for explanation of each type of industrial action.*

Student's answer   The workers could go on strike, which would mean that they would stop work and so no output would be produced. They could then picket the factory by standing outside the gates and trying to stop any delivery lorries or workers going into the factory. This would mean that the business could not produce any toys and the management would be more likely to give in to the union's demands. They could also have an overtime ban.

Examiner's marks and comments

5/6 marks were awarded. 3 for the three types of industrial action and 2 marks for the explanation of the first two types of industrial action. The third type was not explained.

ii) Toys Galore plc recently introduced worker participation by having worker directors. Why might this help to avoid conflict between the workers and the management of Toys Galore plc?

[5 marks]

Marks

2 marks for stating the benefits of worker participation; 2 marks for explaining why it might help to avoid conflict; 1 mark for applying it to Toys Galore plc.

Student's answer

Toys Galore plc produces a lot of products and also exports them. Many decisions will have to be made which will affect the workers. The worker directors will help to increase the flow of information to the other directors concerning the workers' feelings about any changes that are proposed. If these views are taken into account then there is less chance of a decision being made that the workers will not be happy with.

Try to mark this yourself – the examiner's marks and comments are on page 105.

Common misconceptions and errors

Error	Why it is wrong
'Trade unions represent all workers.'	Trade unions only represent the workers who have joined the trade union and not all the other workers.
'Trade unions always cause trouble and call the workers out on strike.'	Trade unions do talk to management in some cases and try to find ways to increase productivity so that there will be an improvement in the working conditions for their members.
'A strike is when all the employees stop work and don't come back to work until the dispute is settled.'	Only trade union members will go out on strike, not the other workers. Also, strikes can be for a short period of time, such as half a day, just to make a point. They do not necessarily go on for very long as workers do not get paid for the time they are on strike. They only get some pay from the union if it has sufficient funds to pay them some money.
'Worker participation is when employees get to tell the management what to do.'	Worker participation is when workers contribute to the decision-making process in some way. They do not take it over.

Try this **a)** Match the type of trade union with the example. [4 marks]

Types of trade union	Examples
Craft union	**i)** The members are all secretaries
Industrial union	**ii)** The members are all different types of workers in the mining industry
General union	**iii)** The members are unskilled and semi-skilled workers in several different industries
White-collar union	**iii)** The members are unskilled and semi-skilled workers in several different industries
	iv) The members are all skilled workers

b) Explain why businesses join employer associations. [6 marks]

Examiner's tip
✓ *Explain three benefits to businesses of joining an employer association.*

c) The workers at P and D Ltd are unhappy because the management wants to change the hours they work. The management wants the workers to work four days at 10 hours per day instead of five days at 8 hours per day. This is so that the workers can be asked to work overtime on the fifth day. Sales of the business's products have been increasing rapidly and more output is needed.

  i) The union wants the workers to take industrial action. Should they go on strike or introduce an overtime ban? Explain your answer.

  [6 marks]

Examiner's tip
✓ *Explain the advantages and disadvantages of strike action and an overtime ban and then decide which would be more effective for the workers at P and D Ltd and why.*

  ii) The management of P and D Ltd has been thinking of introducing worker participation. Suggest three different ways they could use to do this. [6 marks]

Examiner's tip
✓ *Explain three ways of having worker participation, for example, worker directors, works councils, quality circles, or more democratic styles of leadership.*

UNIT 16 The market and marketing

Key objectives

- To understand why marketing is important to a business
- To know the difference between a product-orientated business and a market-orientated business
- To understand what is meant by market segmentation
- To understand why and how a business segments its market
- To know what are the main elements of the marketing mix

Key definitions

Marketing
The management process which identifies customer wants, anticipates their future wants and then goes about satisfying them profitably

→

Marketing helps a business to increase: its sales revenue; profits; market share (or at least maintain it).
It also may want to: improve the image of the product; enter a new market or market segment; develop new products; improve existing products

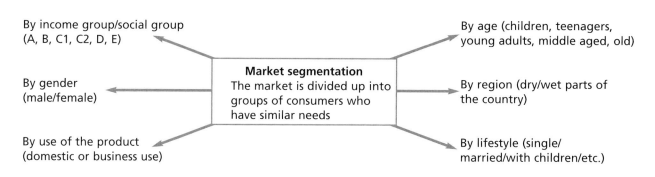

By income group/social group (A, B, C1, C2, D, E)

By gender (male/female)

By use of the product (domestic or business use)

Market segmentation
The market is divided up into groups of consumers who have similar needs

By age (children, teenagers, young adults, middle aged, old)

By region (dry/wet parts of the country)

By lifestyle (single/ married/with children/etc.)

Term	Definition	Example
A market	Where buyers and sellers come together to exchange products for money.	Fruit and vegetable market
Product-orientated business	One whose main focus of activity is on the product itself.	A business which invented a new kitchen tool
Market-orientated business	One which carries out market research to find out consumer wants before a product is developed and produced.	A business which makes chocolate bars finding out what type of chocolate bar appeals to consumers
Marketing budget	A financial plan for the marketing of a product or product range for some specified period of time. It specifies how much money is available to market the product or range, so the marketing department knows how much it can spend.	$500,000 to market a new chocolate bar. The marketing department will then decide which marketing activities it will use to realise its target sales over a specified time period.
Marketing mix	Describes all the activities which go into marketing a product. They are often summarised as the 4 P's: Product, Price, Promotion and Place.	Product – new chocolate bar for small children Price – $0.30 Promotion – advertised on TV during children's programmes Place – sold in supermarkets

Sample questions and answers

Sample question   C & C plc produces washing powder. It has been in business for many years. It started by selling just one type of washing powder, but now it sells many different brands all aimed at different groups of customers (low-income, families with babies, sensitive skin, sports-playing families, people who care for the environment, etc.). When C & C plc was going to introduce a new brand of washing powder it would carry out market research first to find out what consumers wanted from their washing powder. The business would then design a new product to meet these needs. C & C plc has been very successful and seen its sales grow continuously each year.

a) Does C & C plc segment its market? Explain your answer.

[2 marks]

Marks   *1 mark if correctly identifies what is meant by segmenting the market; 1 mark for explaining that C & C plc segments its market.*

Student's answer   Yes – C & C plc sells products to different customers.

Examiner's marks and comments   *The answer is vague. They could have gained the second mark by making it clear that the products are different and targeted towards different customers. 1 mark.*

b) Why does C & C plc do this instead of selling a single product to the whole market?   [4 marks]

Marks   *Explaining why segmentation may be a way of meeting customer needs and increasing sales, 1–2 marks; 1–2 marks for applying this to C & C plc.*

Student's answer   Some businesses aim their products at just one group of customers and not the whole market because this means that the product will satisfy their individual needs. Each brand of C & C washing powder can be bought by a different type of consumer, for example, different income groups or families with babies. Each product is made to appeal to just one of these groups. If each product was aimed at all the groups then it probably wouldn't meet the needs of any particular customer and wouldn't sell so well. Segmenting the market increases sales of the product and, therefore, may result in greater profits.

Examiner's marks and comments   *A clear understanding of market segmentation, which is applied to C & C plc. Full marks.*

c) Do you think C & C plc is a product-orientated business or a market-orientated business? Explain your answer.   [2 marks]

Marks   *1 mark for saying it is a market-orientated business plus 1 mark for explaining why.*

Student's answer   C & C plc is a market-orientated business as market research is carried out to find out what the customer wants and then it makes the new product according to what the customer wants. If the business was product orientated then it would develop a new product and then try to sell it to consumers.

65

The candidate explains that it is a market-orientated business, but does not need to add the second sentence. 2 marks.

Common misconceptions and errors

Error	Why it is wrong
'A market is in a single place.'	A market does not have to be a place. For example, it could be goods sold over the internet.
'Marketing is just about advertising the product.'	Marketing is much more than just advertising or promoting a product or service. It includes consideration of the channel of distribution, the product itself, pricing and packaging.
Developing a marketing mix that does not link together.	A marketing mix must be clearly linked together. For example an expensive high-priced product should have packaging that gives the impression of a high quality product and it should be sold in shops which are used by high-income groups. Promotion needs to emphasise the high quality of the product and ensure that it is advertised in places seen by high-income groups.

● **Try this** Ncube Giftware Ltd manufactures wooden gift items which it exports to European markets. The directors want to expand production. Bafana, the marketing director, says 'The marketing department will play a very important role in helping the business to expand.'

a) Explain three possible objectives of the marketing department at Ncube Giftware Ltd. [6 marks]

b) What are the four elements of the marketing mix? [4 marks]

c) Do you think it is important for the four elements of the marketing mix to link together? Explain your answer. [8 marks]

Examiner's tip
✓ *Try to explain why it might be important to link the elements together and what might happen if the business does not.*

UNIT 17 Market research

Key objectives
- To understand why market research is needed
- To understand the difference between primary and secondary research
- To describe how to carry out market research taking into account sample size, type of sampling method, location and timing of the research
- To evaluate whether the information gathered is accurate

Key definitions

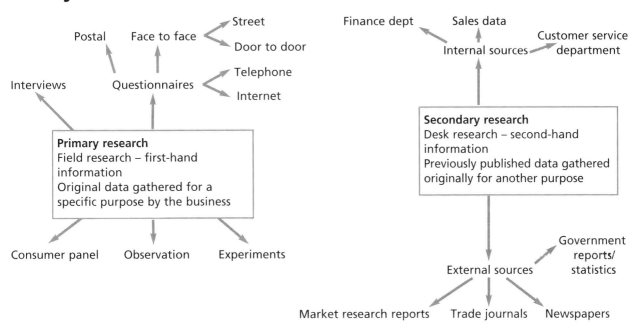

Term	Definition	Examples
Market research	A business finds out consumer wants before a product is developed and produced.	Primary research and secondary research.
Quantitative data	Information about the quantity of something.	How many customers buy cola.
Qualitative data	Information about opinions or judgements.	Why customers like cola.
Random sample	Every member of the population has an even chance of being selected (for example, for a questionnaire or interview).	People are selected at random, for example, every 1000th person in the telephone directory.
Quota sample	People are selected on the basis of certain characteristics, for example, age, gender, income.	A certain number of people are selected for interview or to answer a questionnaire. For example, half should be male and half should be female.

Sample questions and answers

Sample question Khan plc produces chocolate bars and only sells them in its home country. It produces many different brands of chocolate bar which have been selling well for several years. However, one of its brands, called 'Bigga Bars', has seen its sales fall over the last year. Karl, the marketing manager, says 'We must do something to increase total sales revenue from all our products. We must carry out primary and secondary research.'

a) Why might Khan Plc want to carry out market research?

[4 marks]

Marks *1–2 marks for listing one or two reasons why market research might be carried out, for example, to find out why sales have fallen; 1–2 additional marks for explaining these reasons.*

Student's answer Khan plc might carry out market research to see why its product was not what customers wanted. It wants to find out why its product did not meet customer needs, for example, whether the price is too high, or whether any new products have been launched onto the market. When it knows what is wrong with Bigga Bars, it can decide how to make them more appealing to customers or maybe withdraw the product and launch a new one if it is in the decline stage of the product life cycle.

Examiner's marks and comments *This was a good answer with reasons given for carrying out research. These reasons were also explained well. 4 marks.*

b) What is the difference between primary and secondary research?

[4 marks]

Marks *1–2 marks for stating what is meant by primary research or secondary research; 1–2 additional marks for explaining both primary and secondary research and indicating how they are different.*

Student's answer Primary research is first-hand information, whereas secondary research is second-hand information.

Try to mark this answer yourself – the examiner's marks and comments are on page 106.

c) Describe how Khan plc should carry out primary market research before deciding whether to sell a new chocolate bar in a new overseas market. [6 marks]

Marks *Up to 6 marks for describing the process of carrying out a method of primary research. For example, 'The business could design a questionnaire [1]. This would need to be tested to see whether the questions are gathering the correct information the business requires [2]. Care should be taken to ask questions appropriate to the overseas market [3]. The questionnaire should then be carried out after deciding whether it wants a random sample or quota sample [4]. It also needs to decide the sample size to ensure the* *accuracy of the questionnaire [5]. The time, day and place to carry out the questionnaire will be chosen and finally the results will be collated and analysed [6].'*

Student's answer
Primary research is about finding out first-hand information. The company could carry out a questionnaire door to door. Before the product is sold overseas, the company needs to find out about the market and the potential customers. It can then advertise in places where the product will sell and this will mean a lot of sales and increased profits.

Examiner's marks and comments
The candidate has misread the question and said that the company could carry out a questionnaire door to door. The other points are correct, but do not answer the question and therefore this would only gain 1 mark. The rest of the points do not describe how to carry out research.

Common misconceptions and errors

Error	Why it is wrong
'Primary research is information already available.'	Secondary research is information that is already available and gathered for another purpose whereas primary research is original research carried out for a specific purpose.
'Information gathered by primary research is always accurate.'	Poor questions, bad sampling techniques and carrying out the research in the wrong place lead to inaccurate results.
Describing the advantages and disadvantages of primary research when asked to describe how it is carried out.	Need to describe the process of how primary research is carried out rather than discussing this as a method of research.

● **Try this**

a) Give two advantages to a business of using primary market research.

[4 marks]

b) What sources of secondary data are available for a business to use if it wanted to sell a new product in a new overseas market? [3 marks]

c) If primary market research is carried out, explain what the business can do to improve the chances of getting accurate information. [4 marks]

UNIT 18 Presentation of information

Key objectives
- To know how to draw graphs and charts from business data
- To know how to interpret graphs and charts

Sample questions and answers

Sample question XYZ Ltd carried out a questionnaire and here is one of the answers to a question:

What age group are you in?	Number of people
0–20	10
21–35	20
36–50	40
51–65	20
66 +	10

a) Using this information, draw a graph or chart to show the ages of the people who answered the questionnaire. [5 marks]

Marks *1 mark for title; 1 mark for each labelled axis; 2 marks for accurately plotted graph/chart.*

Student's answer

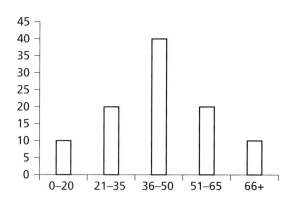

Examiner's marks and comments *The candidate scored 2 marks for a correctly plotted bar chart. The axes were not labelled and there was no title. Total = 2/5 marks.*

b) The graph shows the average wage levels of employees in the company in 2003 and 2004.

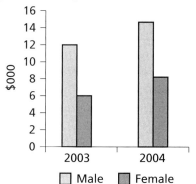

Average annual wages XYZ Ltd 2003 and 2004

● 70

i) Identify the main changes that occurred between 2003 and 2004. [3 marks]

Marks *Identifying that the wages of both men and women increased = 1 mark. Giving the changes in figures = 2 marks.*

ii) If the company employed 30 men in 2003 and 35 men in 2004 calculate the % change in the total male wage costs between 2003 and 2004. [4 marks]

Marks *Total wages for both years calculated = 2 marks. Percentage increase correctly calculated = 2 marks. Up to 3 marks can be awarded for correct method even if there is an error in the calculation.*

Student's answer **i)** Both male and female wages went up. The average male wage increased by $3,000, while the average female wage went up by $2,000.

ii) $12,000 × 30 = $360,000
$15,000 × 35 = $525,000
Increase 525,000 − 360,000 = 165,000
165,000/360,000 = 45.83%

Examiner's marks and comments *The candidate has completed all the answers correctly. Three points were identified – both male and female wages had increased and the increases were given. The second part was correctly calculated. Full marks.*

Common misconceptions and errors

Error

Missing off a title to a graph.

Not labelling axes.

● Try this

a) Using the information in the table below, draw a graph showing the sales of the four main brands produced by this company. [5 marks]

D & D plc – Sales revenue ($millions)

Brands	2002	2003	2004
Chocolate fig bars	3	5	8
Candy bars	3	4	7
Sugar pops	1	4	6
Choco melts	4	5	8

b) The graphs below show information about Miguel's garden business.

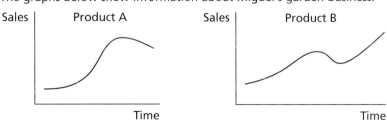

i) Describe what the two graphs show. [4 marks]

ii) Suggest *one* reason for the differences between the two graphs. (See also Unit 19) [3 marks]

UNIT 19 The marketing mix: product and packaging

Key objectives
- To explain why businesses brand products
- To know what factors a business takes into account when branding a product
- To know why packaging is important
- To understand the role that packaging plays in the marketing mix
- To understand how to draw and label a product life cycle
- To understand what happens to prices, profits, sales and promotion as a product passes through the different stages of the life cycle
- To explain how the life cycle can be extended

Key definitions

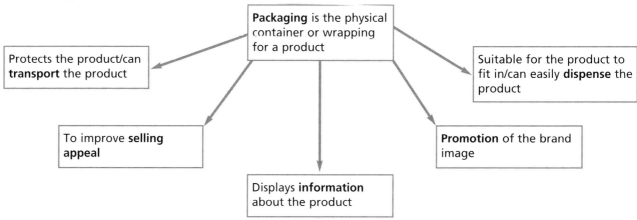

Packaging is the physical container or wrapping for a product

Protects the product/can **transport** the product

Suitable for the product to fit in/can easily **dispense** the product

To improve **selling appeal**

Promotion of the brand image

Displays **information** about the product

Term	Description	Examples
Brand name	The unique name of a product which distinguishes it from other brands. It gives the brand an identity of its own.	Coca-Cola Nike Mars Nissan
Brand loyalty	When customers keep buying a particular brand instead of a competitor's brand.	Customer keeps buying Adidas shoes instead of Nike.
Brand image	The image or identity given to a product which makes it different to its competitors' brands.	Coca-Cola is drunk by people who are trendy and have fun.
Product life cycle	The stages a product will pass through from its introduction, through its growth until it is mature and then finally declines.	The stages are: development introduction growth maturity saturation decline.
Extension strategy	A way of extending the product life cycle when it has reached maturity or saturation stage.	Introduce a new improved version (Playstation 2). Use a new advertising campaign. Sell into new markets. Sell through different outlets. Introduce new variations of the original product/service.

Sample questions and answers

Sample question Mr Patel owns and runs a small private limited company called Patel Enterprises Ltd which manufactures sportswear. The main products are polo shirts, shorts and skirts for younger children who play tennis. The products all have the same brand name, 'Tennis Tiger'. These are high quality clothes which are sold for a high price. The retail outlets which sell these products are specialist sportswear shops, but Patel Enterprises Ltd also sells its products on the internet. The range was launched two years ago and growth in sales has been rapid. However, over the last six months sales have continued to increase, but the increase has been slower than in the previous two years.

a) Why does Patel Enterprises Ltd brand its products? [6 marks]

Marks *1–2 marks for displaying a knowledge of branding; 1–2 marks for applying this to the context of Patel Enterprises Ltd; 1–2 marks for explaining the advantage of branding.*

Student's answer A business brands its products to create a unique identity so that customers will be able to recognise it and buy the products again. 'Tennis Tiger' is the brand name for Patel Enterprises Ltd products. Customers will recognise the brand name and know that these products will be of good quality and it will make them more likely to keep buying the products. Also, if there is a brand logo on the garments then customers will want to buy matching polo shirts and shorts and so the business will increase its sales.

Examiner's marks and comments *This is a good answer with more discussion than necessary to gain full marks. Knowledge of branding is clearly given along with a good application to this case. More than one advantage of branding is also included. Total = 6/6 marks.*

b) What brand image would you suggest for 'Tennis Tiger'? Explain your answer. [4 marks]

Marks *1–2 marks for suggesting a suitable brand image; 1–2 marks for justifying the image in terms of young children.*

Student's answer The brand image should appeal to the target audience. It needs to appeal to people who play tennis and so it should be sporty.

Examiner's marks and comments *This is a general answer. It does link to tennis and sport, but it does not make clear how it would appeal to young children. The student could have discussed the tiger image being cuddly and fun, which would appeal to young children. Total = 2/4 marks.*

c) What stage of the product life cycle do you think 'Tennis Tiger' garments have reached? Justify your choice. [3 marks]

Marks *1 mark for identifying that it has reached the maturity stage of the life cycle; up to 2 marks for justifying why this is the case.*

Student's answer It has reached the maturity stage because sales are still increasing at a rapid rate.

Examiner's marks and comments *1 mark for correctly identifying the stage, but no further marks as the student has not made it clear that sales are increasing at a reducing rate of increase. Total = 1/3 marks.*

d) The increase in the sales of 'Tennis Tiger' products has slowed in the last six months. What do you think the company should do if sales do not increase any more? Explain your answer.

[8 marks]

Marks *1–2 marks for examples of suitable action the business could take; 1–4 marks for showing advantages of these actions explained in terms of the business; 2 marks for justification as to what the business should do.*

Student's answer Patel Enterprises Ltd should increase their advertising of 'Tennis Tiger' clothes to make more consumers aware of the products. They could also run special offers where customers could get a discount on a second garment after they had bought one. These initiatives should encourage sales and see an increase. They could also reduce their prices to encourage more sales, but this may mean using cheaper materials if they are to keep the same profits. A lower price could make consumers think that the garments are not of such a high quality and therefore sales might fall instead of rise. They could also try to sell the clothes in different retail outlets, for example, supermarkets. However, this may not create the right brand image for the clothes. They could also try to sell them abroad.

Try to mark this yourself – the examiner's marks and comments are on page 106.

Common misconceptions and errors

Error	Why it is wrong
'Packaging is just a container for the product.'	Packaging is more than just a container for the product. It can be used to reinforce the branding of the product and promote it. The packaging often makes the product easily recognisable on the shelves and attracts attention.
'In the maturity phase of the product life cycle sales fall.'	In the maturity phase of the product life cycle sales still increase, but only slowly.
'After the saturation phase of the product life cycle, a product's sales will always fall.'	After the saturation phase of the product life cycle, sales will fall if it moves into the decline phase. However, if the business successfully uses extension strategies then the life of the product will be extended and sales may increase.

● **Try this**   Peacock plc manufactures and sells soft drinks. The main brand it sells is bought by sports players. The outer packaging of the drink is plain black and some customers have complained that it is difficult to drink from the container. The marketing manager, Sheena, thinks that some changes need to be made to the packaging to improve sales of the drink.

a) What functions does packaging perform for the sports drink produced by Peacock plc? [5 marks]

> **Examiner's tip**
> ✓ Make sure you apply your answer to the sports drink in the case.

b) What factors should Sheena take into account when changing the packaging for this sports drink? [6 marks]

> **Examiner's tip**
> ✓ Do not describe the changes she should make.

c) Draw and label the stages of a typical product life cycle on a graph. [4 marks]

> **Examiner's tip**
> ✓ Do not forget to label the axes.

d) Pricing is a very important element in the marketing mix of a business. How and why might a business change its prices during the stages of a typical life cycle? (See also Unit 20). [6 marks]

> **Examiner's tip**
> ✓ Describe the change and then say what should happen as a result of the change.

e) Why do some products have much longer life cycles than others? Give examples to illustrate your answer. [4 marks]

UNIT 20 The marketing mix: price

Key objectives

- To explain what affects demand and supply
- To understand what is meant by elastic and inelastic demand for a product
- To explain what happens to demand for a product if the price increases or decreases when demand is elastic or inelastic
- To understand the different pricing strategies and explain when they would be suitable to use

Key definitions

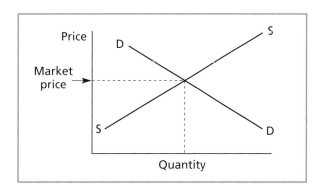

Supply is determined by the decisions of producers: affected by price, the cost of producing the goods, taxes/subsidies, improvements in technology, climate

Demand is determined by the decisions of consumers: affected by price, price of substitute products, taste and fashion, advertising, consumers' income, price of complementary products

Pricing strategy	Definition	Price charged
Cost-plus pricing	The cost of manufacturing the product plus a profit mark-up	Cost = $100 + 50% profit Price = $150
Penetration pricing	When the price is set lower than the competitors' prices in order to be able to enter a new market.	Competitors' prices = $10 This price = $9.50
Price skimming	A high price is set for a new product on the market.	New product price = $50 No near substitute on the market
Competitive pricing	The product is priced in line with or just below competitors' prices to try to capture more of the market.	Competitors' prices = $20–$23 This product price = $22
Promotional pricing	When a product is sold at a very low price for a short period of time.	Competitors' prices = $10 This product = $7 for a limited period of time
Psychological pricing	When particular attention is paid to the effect that the price of a product will have upon the customers' perceptions of the product.	Price = $9.99
Price elastic demand	Demand changes by a greater proportion than price change.	
Price inelastic demand	Demand changes by a smaller proportion than price change.	

Sample questions and answers

Sample question Luxury Leisure plc owns and runs several leisure centres in the capital city of country X. The centres are expensive to join, but are at a similar price to other luxury centres in the city. They want to encourage more people to become members, so have advertised a special low rate to join the leisure centre for a limited time in order to encourage additional members. Last year Luxury Leisure plc put its prices up from $40 per month to $50 per month, but found that membership fell by 15%.

a) Identify two pricing strategies that are being used by Luxury Leisure plc. [2 marks]

Marks *1 mark for each correct answer – competitive pricing and promotional pricing.*

Student's answer Competitive pricing and penetration pricing.

Examiner's marks and comments *The first answer is correct, but the second one is not correct as the service is not new and not trying to get into a new market. Total = 1 mark.*

b) Explain one other pricing strategy Luxury Leisure plc could use and why it might use it. [3 marks]

Marks *1 mark for a suitable strategy; up to 2 marks for explaining why it might be suitable for this business to use.*

Student's answer It could use cost-plus pricing as this would ensure that all the costs were covered.

Examiner's marks and comments *1 mark for a suitable method and 1 mark for the explanation. Total = 2/3 marks as the student did not go on to explain the answer in detail.*

c) Using the information in the case study above, should Luxury Leisure plc have put its prices up from $40 to $50 per month? Explain your answer. [6 marks]

Marks *2 marks for identifying that demand is inelastic; 2 marks for explaining the effects of the change; 2 marks for making a judgement.*

Student's answer The price was increased by $10, a 25% increase. This means that demand is inelastic. The business should have put its prices up, as this would mean that the company would increase its sales revenue and possibly its profits.

Try to mark this yourself – the examiner's marks and comments are on page 107.

Common misconceptions and errors

Error	Why it is wrong
'Sugar is an inelastic product.'	As sugar is a basic necessity, **demand** for sugar could be said to be inelastic. The product itself is not inelastic.
'Price skimming is where the product is priced below the prices of competitors.'	Price skimming is where a new product enters a market at a high price. It is usually a new invention, or a new development of an old product, and therefore it can be sold on the market at a high price and people will pay this because of the novelty factor.
'Putting prices down will always gain increased sales.'	Reducing prices will sometimes cause sales to fall if the product has an image of being high quality. Customers may think that the quality is lower as the price is now lower and not buy it.

● **Try this** Acmo Oil plc is a multi-national oil company. It extracts oil, refines it and also owns the petrol stations where its petrol is sold. Many of the petrol stations also have shops that sell food, drinks, maps and gift items. The gift items are also sold in many other local shops.

a) Would this business's revenue be likely to increase if it were to cut petrol prices? Explain your answer giving reasons. [4 marks]

> **Examiner's tip**
> ✓ Think about whether demand is elastic or inelastic. Would customers be sensitive to price reductions or not, and would they buy a lot more or would there be just a small percentage increase in sales?

b) Often Acmo's shops reduce their prices of giftware at certain times of the year. Why do you think they do this? [4 marks]

c) Discuss the factors that affect which pricing strategy for giftware this business uses? [8 marks]

> **Examiner's tip**
> ✓ Think about the factors that influence whether the business should use competitive pricing, price skimming, etc. Examples of factors might include: nearby competitors; at what stage of the product life cycle the products are; costs of production; whether product is high quality.

UNIT 21 The marketing mix: promotion

Key objectives

- To understand that there are four types of promotion and to understand when they are used
- To understand the factors that affect the types of advertising to use
- To know what is meant by the target audience
- To explain when to use the different types of promotion
- To explain when to use personal selling
- To explain the role of PR (public relations) in business
- To know the importance of customer service

Key definitions

Advertisements
Including television, radio, newspapers and magazines, posters/billboards, cinemas, leaflets/direct mail, internet

Promotional offers
Price reductions, gifts, point-of-sale display and demonstration, after-sales service, free samples, competitions, money-off coupons

Types of promotion

Personal selling
Goods sold straight to the customer, for example, where customers may need advice or where the exact nature of the product can vary

Public relations
This is concerned with promoting a good image for the business. Often takes the form of sponsoring an event

Term	Definition	Examples
Persuasive advertising	Advertising or promotion which is trying to persuade the consumer that they really need the product and should buy it.	'Buy XYZ – it's the best!'
Informative advertising	The emphasis of advertising or sales promotion is to give full information about the product.	'XYZ is a new product and it will carry out the functions five times faster than the old product.'
Target audience	The people who are the potential consumers of the product or service.	Children are the target audience for toys.
Customer service	Concerned with keeping customers happy by making them feel important and building a good relationship between the business and its customers.	Giving advice about the product; delivering goods for consumers; providing credit facilities; providing product information; after-sales service.

Sample questions and answers

Sample question Party Extraordinaire is a partnership business that was formed five years ago. It organises parties for young children for birthdays and other special celebrations. The business has been very successful and wants to expand. It currently advertises in local newspapers and puts up posters in local toy shops and children's clothes shops. Customers often use the business again and it also gets bookings from customers telling their friends about the business. It wants to expand into organising parties for adults.

a) Why does Party Extraordinaire advertise in this way?   [2 marks]

Marks *2 marks for an explanation.*

Student's answer Party Extraordinaire advertises in local newspapers because local people will use its service and see the adverts. It also puts up posters in toy shops and children's clothes shops, so again people with children are likely to go to these places, see the business's adverts and might therefore use its services.

Examiner's marks and comments *A good answer. The student correctly identifies where the business advertises and why it should be effective, as the target audience will see the advertisements. Full marks.*

b) Party Extraordinaire decides to expand into organising parties for adults. Suggest three suitable ways it could promote the new service. Justify your choice.   [9 marks]

Marks *1 mark for each suitable way of promoting the business (3 maximum); up to 2 marks for justifying why each way would be effective in the context of this business (6 maximum).*

Student's answer Party Extraordinaire could offer a promotion whereby, if the customer books one party, then a second is given at a reduced price. This would encourage customers to come back and book more parties. The business could advertise in the local newspapers, as local adults would see an advert there. Finally, customers could be entered in a competition if they booked a party.

Try to mark this yourself – the examiner's marks and comments are on page 107.

c) Party Extraordinaire is designing a new poster to put in toy shops. Discuss whether the poster should use mainly informative or persuasive advertising.   [4 marks]

Marks *2 marks for discussing the advantages/disadvantages of informative advertising; 2 marks for explaining the advantages/disadvantages of persuasive advertising; 2 marks for making a judgement as to which one the business should use.*

Student's answer The poster could be persuasive, which would mean that the poster would make the parties sound really good and make customers want to book one. This type of advertising is effective when people need to be encouraged to book a party which they might otherwise not bother to do. Customers need to think that it is good value for money. I think they should use persuasive advertising, as it will encourage more people to book parties.

Examiner's marks and comments

2 marks for explaining the advantages of persuasive advertising and 1 mark for making a judgement. However, the student has not explained informative advertising and so full marks cannot be awarded. 3/6 marks.

Common misconceptions and errors

Error	Why it is wrong
'Promotion only includes advertising.'	Promotion includes advertising but also other types of promotion such as competitions.
'Television is always a good way to advertise.'	Television is expensive and, depending on the time adverts are shown, they may not be seen by the target audience.
'Increased advertising expenditure always increases sales.'	Just because more money is spent on advertising does not mean that it will be effective and persuade more customers to buy the product. The advertising might be in the wrong places to be seen by the target audience or competitors could be spending more on advertising as well.
'Personal selling is where you have a shop assistant serving customers.'	Selling in a shop is not really what personal selling means, this is just serving customers and is not a form of promotion. Personal selling is where the business promotes the business by visiting its customers and discussing their individual needs. For example, a representative of a building company visiting a customer to discuss what they want. It is usually used where an individual product or service is being sold.

● **Try this**   Music Mania is a shop which sells music CDs. It is located in a large shopping centre in the city centre. The CDs it sells are by bands and singers who appeal to teenagers. It has been in business for five years and wants to expand.

a) Identify the target audience for Music Mania.   [1 mark]

b) The management of Music Mania wants to expand. It needs to decide whether to spend more on advertising or to sell a wider range of music CDs which appeal to different age groups. What factors should influence the decision?   [6 marks]

> **Examiner's tip**
> ✓ *Consider factors like the cost, trends in spending habits, which option is most likely to increase profits, and what type of customers use the shopping centre.*

c) Music Mania has decided to sell classical music including opera music. Explain the factors this business should take into account when deciding which form of promotion to use. [8 marks]

Examiner's tip

✓ *Think about the target audience – hence where Music Mania should advertise and cost of advertising, different forms of promotion available, for example, competitions, whether to use PR, etc.*

d) Music Mania would not use personal selling. Give an example of a business that you think would use personal selling. Justify your choice of example. [4 marks]

UNIT 22 The marketing mix: place

Key objectives
- To understand the different channels of distribution
- To understand the role of the wholesaler
- To select the most appropriate channel of distribution for a given product
- To select the most appropriate method of transporting goods for a given product

Key definitions
A **channel of distribution** is the means by which a product is passed from the place where it is produced to the customer or consumer. There are four main channels used by business as follows:

Channel of distribution				Explanation/examples
Producer →	→	→	Consumer	Direct selling of products such as components to businesses, new windows for a house, products sold over the internet (known as e-commerce).
Producer →	→	Retailer	Consumer	Products are sold in bulk to retailers, such as food products to supermarkets, or specialist/expensive products, such as jewellery.
Producer →	**Wholesaler:** Buys in large quantities from manufacturer and sells in small quantities to small retailers.	Retailer	Consumer	This is where the wholesaler breaks bulk, such as for some food products.
Producer	**Agent:** Independent person or business who deals with the sales and distribution of a product(s).	Wholesaler	Retailer	Consumer	When products are exported, the manufacturer sometimes uses an agent in the other country. The agent then sells the product(s) on behalf of the manufacturer.

Method of transportation is the type of transport that the manufacturer uses to deliver the products to the market. The most common methods are road haulage (lorries), railways, canal or river, sea freight, air freight and pipelines. Generally, the slower the form of transport the cheaper it will be.

Sample questions and answers

Sample questions   1) What are the advantages to a producer of using a channel of distribution as shown below?   [4 marks]

Producer → wholesaler → retailer → consumer

Marks   *1–2 marks for each advantage to the producer.*

Student's answer The producer can sell in bulk to the wholesaler and therefore does not have to spend money storing the products in the warehouse. The cost of distribution will be lower, as the producer only has to deliver to the wholesaler and not to many different retailers.

Examiner's marks and comments *Two good explanations of advantages to the producer – full marks.*

2) C & D plc produces computer games designed to be played on PCs. It is a large business based in Brazil, but sells its games in many different countries. It has just developed a new computer game for teenage children. This new game is to be sold in one of the business's South East Asian markets to see how popular it is before launching it in all the different countries the business sells to.

　i) What channel of distribution would you suggest that the company uses for its new game? Justify your choice. [4 marks]

Marks *1 mark for an explanation of a suitable channel of distribution; 3 marks for explanation of why this channel would be suitable.*

Student's answer The manufacturer should sell it to a computer game retailer and then on to the customer. This would be a good channel of distribution to use because the customer would need advice about the game and the retailer could be a specialist computer type of shop. If the games were sold to a wholesaler, the correct advice might not get to the customer. Also, wholesalers would not buy these games in bulk if most of their retail customers were small shops which sold food and would not be interested in stocking computer games.

Examiner's marks and comments *A good answer – a suitable channel was suggested (although it was possible to argue that other channels of distribution might be suitable) and then the channel was justified in terms of selling to a retailer and not using a wholesaler. Even though some of the points might not always be true in some countries, the answer was a correct justification for selling straight to retailers and not through wholesalers. Full marks.*

　ii) What factors should C & D plc consider when deciding the marketing mix for its new computer game? [8 marks]

Marks *2 marks for listing up to two or more factors; 4 marks for explaining up to two or more factors; 2 marks for the answer being applied to the computer games market.*

Student's answer C & D plc will firstly have to consider who its target market is for the new game. As it is teenagers, the business will have to design a game that will appeal to this group of consumers. The advertising and promotions will have to be in places that will be seen by teenagers and sold in shops teenagers visit. C & D plc needs to consider how large its advertising budget for promoting the new game will be. If it is not very large then the business will have to think carefully about where it advertises as it will soon run out of money. TV advertising may not be possible if the budget is small. What competitors do will also have to be taken into account. If competitors sell their computer games in certain shops then C & D plc may also have to sell its new game in these same shops as this will be where teenagers will go to buy games and will see the new game and buy it. C & D plc will also need to advertise in similar places to its competitors so that teenagers will see the adverts. The pricing strategy may have to be competitive pricing if there are already a lot of competitors selling similar games, or penetration pricing if the business needs to break into this market.

Try to mark this yourself – the examiner's marks and comments are on page 107.

Common misconceptions and errors

Error	Why it is wrong
'Place is where the product is sold.'	Place is making the product available where and when the customer wants to buy and is not just the shop used to sell the product.
'Retailers break bulk.'	A wholesaler breaks bulk by buying from the manufacturer in large quantities and dividing up the product into smaller quantities to sell to small retailers.
'Selling through a wholesaler makes products more expensive than if they are sold directly to a retailer.'	A wholesaler can be cheaper to buy from because they buy in such large quantities from manufacturers they get discounts and their delivery and administration costs can be much lower.
'Road transport is always the best to use.'	Road transport can be more expensive and slower than other forms of transport – it depends on the product being delivered.

● **Try this**   a) Put the following products in the suitable channels of distribution:

[4 marks]

- tins of fruit
- shoes (exported)
- wedding cakes
- new cars.

Product

i) Producer	→	→	→	Consumer
ii) Producer	→	→	Retailer	Consumer
iii) Producer	→	Wholesaler	Retailer	Consumer
iv) Producer	Agent	Wholesaler	Retailer	Consumer

b) D & E is a food processing business. The directors are thinking about ending sales of their ready made meals to a retail chain of supermarkets and selling them to an airline for in-flight meals. What are the advantages and disadvantages of doing this?   [10 marks]

c) Monay Ltd was set up ten years ago. It started making wooden tables, but slowly expanded and now makes several different types of furniture. Sales of its products have kept growing and profits have increased rapidly. The directors of Monay Ltd want to expand into the manufacture of quality dining tables and chairs, which it wants to sell to high-income consumers.

Suggest a marketing mix that this business could use if it introduces quality dining tables and chairs.   [12 marks]

d) Why might a different marketing mix be used for the same product in different countries?   [8 marks]

UNIT 23 Factors affecting production

Key objectives

- To understand what is meant by value added
- To be able to identify what factors may increase productivity
- To understand the different methods of production and when they would be used
- To understand the effects of new technology on both the business and its employees
- To identify the different ways of ensuring quality of the product or service

Key definitions

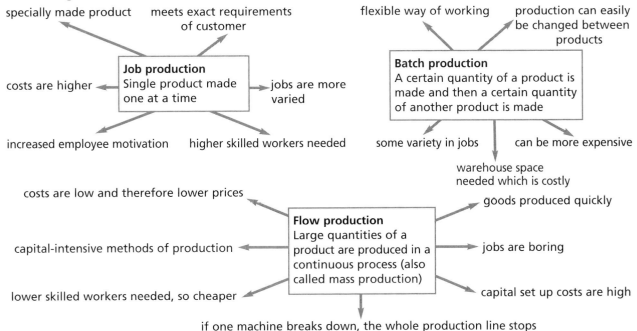

specially made product   meets exact requirements of customer

flexible way of working   production can easily be changed between products

Job production
Single product made one at a time

costs are higher   jobs are more varied

Batch production
A certain quantity of a product is made and then a certain quantity of another product is made

some variety in jobs   can be more expensive

increased employee motivation   higher skilled workers needed

warehouse space needed which is costly

costs are low and therefore lower prices

goods produced quickly

capital-intensive methods of production

Flow production
Large quantities of a product are produced in a continuous process (also called mass production)

jobs are boring

lower skilled workers needed, so cheaper

capital set up costs are high

if one machine breaks down, the whole production line stops

Term	Explanation	Examples
Value added	Difference between the selling price and the cost of inputs.	Product sells for $10; cost of inputs $2 per unit; value added = $8
Labour productivity	Output measured against the labour input used to produce it.	$\dfrac{\text{Output (over a given period of time)}}{\text{Number of employees}}$
Stock control	There should always be sufficient stock to meet demand. This is checked both in the production and in the shops.	See figure below.
Lean production	Techniques used by a business to cut down on any waste and therefore increase efficiency.	Reduce the time taken for a product to be developed; reduce any waste in the production process.

Stock levels — Maximum stock level — Reorder level — Minimum stock level — Time

Term	Explanation	Examples
Quality control	Inspectors check the finished goods to detect any faulty ones.	Sample one in every 100 products produced to make sure none is faulty.
Quality assurance	There is inspection both during and after production and tries to stop any faults from happening in the first place. Requires team working from the employees.	All the production workers check their part of the process and make sure there are no faulty components or faulty finished products.

Sample questions and answers

Sample question Sita Ltd produces clothes for babies. It has been in business for ten years and has seen sales increase rapidly throughout this time. It employs 50 production workers who use sewing machines. The production manager wants to introduce new sewing machines that are twice as fast as the old ones. It will allow the business to produce higher quality baby clothes as well as gain from other benefits of new technology. The average selling price of an item of clothing is $10 with material costing $1. However, with new machines it will allow the selling price to increase to $15 and material will only cost $2.

a) What will happen to the value added of the average product if new technology is introduced? [3 marks]

Marks *2 marks for value added $10 − $1 = $9 and $15 − $2 = $13.*
3 marks in total for a correct answer: new technology $13 − $9 = $4.

Student's answer $10 − $1 = $9 and $15 − $2 = $13. Value added increases by $3.

Examiner's marks and comments *Correct method, incorrect answer. 2/3 marks.*

b) Why might the production manager want to introduce new technology at Sita Ltd? [8 marks]

Marks *Up to 3 marks for lists of why new technology is an advantage; up to 3 marks for explanation of advantages of new technology; 2 marks for applying the answer to this business.*

Student's answer New technology will allow Sita Ltd to produce more high quality garments. As productivity will increase, it may be able to decrease the number of employees and therefore production wages will be reduced and even though the new technology will cost a lot of money to buy, it may increase profits.

Examiner's marks and comments *The answer is in the context of Sita Ltd and so 2 application marks were gained; 1 mark for the first advantage and 3 marks for the second advantage as it is explained. Total = 6/8 marks. Explanation of the first or third point would have gained full marks – a good answer.*

c) Sita Ltd uses batch production in the production of baby clothes.
i) What is meant by batch production? [2 marks]

Marks *2 marks for a clear definition; 1 mark for a vague answer.*

Student's answer   Batch production is where an amount of a particular product is produced and then an amount of another product is produced.

Try to mark this yourself – the examiner's marks and comments are on page 108.

   ii) Why does Sita Ltd use batch production and not flow production? [6 marks]

Marks   *2 marks for advantages of batch production or disadvantages of flow production; 2 additional marks for explanation of these advantages/disadvantages; 2 marks if applied to Sita Ltd.*

Student's answer   Sita Ltd uses batch production because it does not sell enough baby clothes to produce a large quantity as there is not enough demand. Also these kinds of products come in many diffcrent styles and sizes and not just one basic product so again the business will need to produce so many of one size, so many of another size, etc. Flow production would mean a very large quantity of a single garment would be made and Sita Ltd wouldn't be able to sell them all.

Examiner's marks and comments   *A good answer, although there is some repetition at the end. Well applied to the case. Full marks.*

Common misconceptions and errors

Error	Why it is wrong
'Value added is profit made.' (Also in Unit 1)	Value added is not just profit, it is the selling price minus the cost of inputs.
'Increased productivity means that production increases.'	Productivity usually refers to an increase in output per worker which may mean an increase in output overall or it may not.
'Flow production is where a lot of production of one product is produced and then quite a lot of production of another product is made.'	Flow production is where large quantities are produced in a continuous process. A large quantity of a standardised product is produced.
'Quality control is making sure a product is of the highest quality.'	Quality control is where products are checked to make sure there are no faults with the products and they meet the standards expected for that product. It does not mean the product is of high quality just that it does not have any defects.
'New technology always means jobs are lost.'	When new technology is introduced some jobs may be lost as machines may now do particular jobs. However, other jobs may now be created, for example, computer programmers, operators of the new equipment, maintenance jobs.

● **Try this**

a) Medic Supplies plc produces equipment for hospitals. Some of the equipment it sells is designed to a particular hospital's specification and is built to their order, such as machines which scan patients' whole bodies. Other equipment is produced continuously, such as bandages.

   i) What two methods of production does Medic Supplies plc use?

   [2 marks]

   ii) Why is quality control or quality assurance so important to Medic Supplies plc? [4 marks]

> **Examiner's tip**
> ✓ Explain what is meant by quality control or quality assurance – you do not need to do both. Apply your answer to Medic Supplies plc.

   iii) Explain how Medic Supplies plc can use stock control to make sure it never runs out of raw materials when producing bandages.

   [6 marks]

> **Examiner's tip**
> ✓ Explain the process of stock control and how it ensures that raw materials should always be available so production can take place.

   iv) The directors at Medic Supplies plc have been advised to introduce lean production techniques. Describe what is meant by 'lean production' and how it might be used at Medic Supplies plc.

   [6 marks]

b) Telesales Services Ltd was set up four years ago. It processes orders for several small businesses in a city. It takes orders from customers and then passes these back to the small business so that the item(s) can be delivered. It introduced on-line ordering one year ago and has found that this side of the business has grown very rapidly. However, the telephone ordering side of the business has fallen slightly.

   i) 'It is four times cheaper to process an order on-line than over the telephone,' says Miguel, the Managing Director. Why do you think this is true? Explain your answer. [6 marks]

> **Examiner's tip**
> ✓ Explain the cost savings of using computers to take orders instead of people.

   ii) Explain why the employees might be worried about the trend in increased on-line ordering and fewer telephone orders at Telesales Services Ltd. [4 marks]

> **Examiner's tip**
> ✓ Explain the possible effects on the number and types of jobs at the company.

UNIT 24 Factors affecting location

Key objectives

- To understand the factors that affect the location of a manufacturing business
- To understand the factors that affect the location of a retailing business
- To understand the factors that affect the relocation of a business
- To understand the factors that affect the location of a service sector business

Key definitions

Factors affecting the location of these different businesses:

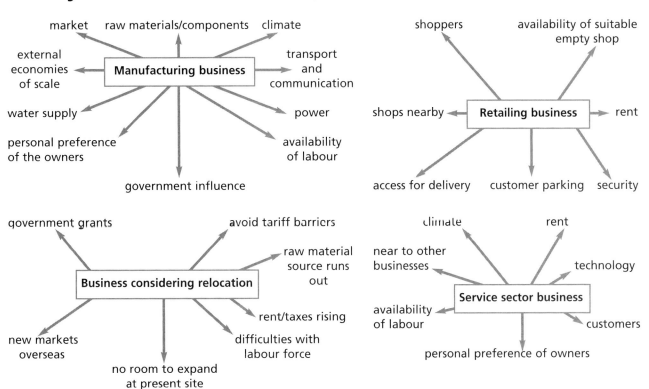

Sample questions and answers

Sample questions

1) Better Burgers is a fast food chain. It has fast food outlets in many different countries and is considering opening a new outlet in a city centre. Discuss what would be the most important factors when deciding on where to locate this outlet.

[10 marks]

Marks *1–4 marks for listing/explaining factors that would affect location decisions; 2 marks for application to fast food outlets; 1–4 marks for explaining which would be the most important factors.*

Student's answer Better Burgers needs to find a site that is in the centre of the city. It should be where there are lots of shoppers who would be likely to use the fast food outlet. The location should also be near places for customers to park their cars. The rent to be paid on the premises should be considered, as it will be very high in the city centre compared with the edge of the city. Delivery vehicles will need to be able to get to the outlet so that they can deliver food. An empty shop or building will have to be looked for and the security of the area should be taken into account. If there are a lot of robberies in the area, it might not be the best of locations. The kind of shops and restaurants nearby is an important factor to consider, as they will attract shoppers to the area who might then eat at the outlet. The most important factor is the number of customers there will be in the area. The outlet needs to be in the centre of the city to make sure it attracts a lot of customers. Then the amount of rent paid will not be very important as the outlet will make a lot of sales to pay the rent easily. Access by delivery vehicles is less important as they will be able to get the food to the outlet easily by trolley. Obviously, an empty shop is needed, but it does not matter if it is not in the right area.

Examiner's marks and comments *10 marks. The factors were discussed and applied to this scenario. The importance of the factors was also discussed.*

2) A car sales outlet wants to open in the city. Why would its location be different to a jewellery shop? Explain your answer.

[8 marks]

Marks *3 marks for explaining the factors that affect the location of a jewellery shop; 3 marks for explaining the factors that affect the location of a car sales outlet; 2 marks for making the differences clear.*

Student's answer A jewellery shop would need to be on a high street or main road where a lot of people would pass by and look in the shop window. It needs to be in a secure area, so that it is at less risk of theft. The shop could be located near other jewellery shops to attract people coming to the area to buy jewellery.

　　The car sales outlet needs a lot of space to park all the cars for sale. The rent should not be too high as the premises will take up a large area, which will make it expensive. Access for customer parking is important because customers are likely to drive up in their cars and need to park so they can look at the cars for sale. As long as cars can get in and out, access for delivery shouldn't be important.

Examiner's marks and comments *Comparisons are not made, even though factors affecting both types of shop are explained. Therefore 6/8 marks were awarded. Clear comparisons are needed for full marks.*

3) A company that cleans offices needs to decide where to locate its own office staff. Why might it not locate its own offices in the city centre? [6 marks]

Marks *Up to 3 marks for listing disadvantages of locating in the city centre; up to 3 marks for explaining these disadvantages.*

Student's answer The city centre is expensive in terms of rent of premises. It is an area that a lot of businesses want to locate in and this will drive up the rent to be paid. It is difficult and expensive to park cars in the city centre. It takes a lot of time for employees to get to work in the city centre. The offices do not need to be located where there are a lot of people.

Try to mark this yourself – the examiner's marks and comments are on page 108.

Try to mark this yourself – the examiner's marks and comments are on page 108.

Common misconceptions and errors

Error	Why it is wrong
'Businesses need to be near the raw material source.'	Businesses only need to be near their raw materials if they are a manufacturing business and produce a lot of waste. It is not so important to be near the raw material source with today's improved transport links.
'It is always better to locate near to customers.'	Many businesses locate where their costs will be low. This may be in another country where wages are low. It may not be near to customers.
'The internet has not affected where businesses locate.'	Businesses that use the internet to sell their products do not need to be near to customers any more, as they receive their orders over the internet and then post the goods to customers. The business can locate anywhere.

● Try this

a) M and T plc manufactures chocolates. It wants to set up a new factory making chocolates. The business employs a lot of workers and many of them need to be qualified in chocolate making. The cocoa used to make the chocolate is imported.

    i) Select three factors that would affect the location of this business and explain why they are important. [6 marks]

    ii) This business has started to sell an increasing quantity of its chocolates in an overseas market. The Managing Director is thinking of moving the manufacture of the chocolates to this overseas market. Discuss what factors he should take into account when deciding whether to move the factory abroad. [10 marks]

> **Examiner's tip**
> ✓ *Consider the market, costs of setting up a new factory, costs of running a factory in this overseas market.*

b) Governments do not usually leave the location decisions totally to businesses themselves. Explain why you think this is the case.   [6 marks]

> **Examiner's tip**
> ✓ *Explain the disadvantages of businesses choosing to locate where they want to without any consideration of the local population or environment.*

c) DD Ltd is a business that stocks and sells sports clothes over the internet. Discuss whether you think the location of the business is important.

[6 marks]

UNIT 25 Business in the international community

Key objectives
- To understand that business success can be influenced by international factors
- To explain how exchange rates can have an impact on businesses that import and export
- To understand what globalisation is and why it is increasing
- To explain the effect that multinational businesses can have on a country

Key definitions

Term	Definition	Examples
Imports	Products bought by a country from other countries.	Spain imports oil from Saudi Arabia, Saudi Arabia imports cars from Germany.
Exports	Products sold from a country to other countries.	Give two examples of important exports from your own country.
Exchange rate	The price of one currency in terms of another.	The exchange rate for £ in terms of the euro was £1:1.45€ in May 2004. Find out the exchange rate for your country's currency in terms of the US$.
Currency appreciation	When the currency buys more of another currency than before, its value rises.	OLD: £1:$1 NEW: £1:$1.50 £ has appreciated
Currency depreciation	When the currency buys less of another currency than before, its value falls.	OLD: 1€:$1 NEW: 1€:$0.80 € has depreciated
Common (single) currency	When a group of countries agree to use the same currency.	The euro is used by many members of the European Union.
Tariff	A tax on imports to make them less competitive with domestically produced products.	Try to find out about a tariff put on an import into your country and make a note.
Quota	A maximum limit on the quantity of imported goods allowed into a country.	Does your country have any import quotas? Try to find out one such quota and make a note.
Globalisation	The increase in international trade and competition, as shown by the growth of multinational corporations.	World trade is growing at over 10% each year. Tarrifs and quotas are being reduced.
Multinational corporations	Businesses that have operations in more than one country.	Coca-Cola, McDonalds, Ikea (furniture), Canon (copiers and cameras).
Economic union	Agreements between countries to trade freely with each other and have common economic institutions.	The European Union (EU).

Sample questions and answers

Sample question Three countries, X, Y and Z, trade with each other. The government of Country X is worried about the high level of imports from the other two countries. The government of Country Y wants to encourage the other countries to join a common currency. The currency of Country Z has recently appreciated against the currencies of the other two countries.

a) State *one* way in which Country X could reduce imports from the other two countries. [1 mark]

Marks *1 mark for either import tariff or import quota.*

Student's answer Tariffs on imports is one way.

Examiner's marks and comments *1 mark.*

b) Explain *two* ways in which businesses in Country X might be affected by the government reducing imports. [4 marks]

Marks *1 mark for identifying each factor plus 1 further mark for some development of each factor.*

Student's answer If imports were reduced then consumers might start buying more products from businesses in Country X. This would increase sales. Also, a reduced supply of imports could increase prices.

Examiner's marks and comments *This answer is worth 3 marks. The first point is a good one and the effect on businesses is briefly explained. The second point is only identified and gains 1 mark. The student should have explained the possible effect on business of higher import prices, for example, if a business in Country X imports important materials then a price increase would raise its costs. This could lead to lower profits.*

c) Do you think that businesses in these three countries would benefit from a common (single) currency? Explain your answer. [6 marks]

Marks *1 mark for definition, up to 5 marks for giving a balanced discussion; maximum of 4 if only one side of argument is given.*

Student's answer A single currency is when several countries agree to use the same money so that when they trade the same money can be used. This would benefit businesses. It would mean that companies would not have to convert money into foreign currency if they were buying imports. This would save on currency exchange costs. A common currency also means that they could just print one price list for all three countries which would save on costs.
There are possible drawbacks too though.

Examiner's marks and comments *4 marks. This is a good, though one-sided, answer. There is no evaluation of the benefits, so it cannot earn more than 4 marks. The student should have explained briefly two points against a common currency. For example, it will be easier for consumers to compare prices and competition may increase due to the ease of selling to other countries.*

d) i) Complete this table with an exchange rate for Country Z's currency (Yen) in 2005 showing an appreciation compared to the $. [1 mark]

2004	1 Yen : $2
2005	1 Yen : ....

Marks *1 mark for correct answer (any rate over $2).*

Student's answer $2.50

Examiner's marks and comments *Yes, the student understands that an appreciation means that a currency unit buys more of another currency than before. 1 mark.*

ii) Explain *one* effect of this appreciation on exporters in Country Z. [4 marks]

Marks *2 marks for explaining that export prices could rise; 2 marks for development – it could lead to lower demand for exports and lower profits from exporting.*

Student's answer When a currency appreciates it makes imports cheaper and exports more expensive. This means that exporters in Country Z will find it more difficult to sell goods to other countries. Exporting will become more difficult and less profitable.

Try to mark this yourself – the examiner's marks and comments are on page 109.

Common misconceptions and errors

Error	Why it is wrong
'International trade is bad for business as it leads to more competition.'	Although trading with other countries can increase competition, businesses also have much larger markets and can often purchase supplies cheaply from other countries.
'A business can easily sell its products to other countries.'	Selling to other countries is not always easy. Products and marketing may need to be changed to meet local market conditions, for example.
'Multinationals sell products in more than one country.'	To be termed a multinational, a business should have production operations in more than one country.

● **Try this** Zircon plc manufactures chemicals for industry. Currently it only operates in one country. Zircon is planning to set up another chemical factory in Country X, which has a rapidly expanding economy. Country X has high tariffs on all imports. The Managing Director of Zircon has asked the government of Country X for permission to build the factory. The government and trade unions are very interested in the plan. Greenworld, a local environmental group, is against the plan.

a) Explain *two* reasons why Zircon is planning to become a multinational.

[4 marks]

b) List *two* problems Zircon might face when operating in another country.

[2 marks]

c) Evaluate whether the government of Country X should allow Zircon to build the new chemical factory. [8 marks]

Examiner's tip

✓ *Consider the advantages and disadvantages to the country of Zircon's new factory, then come to an overall conclusion.*

Answers

UNIT 1 The purpose of business activity

Sample questions and answers

b) Examiner's marks and comments: This answer shows a good understanding of division of labour (1 mark) and the possible benefits to ARC (3 marks). The disadvantages are less detailed (1 mark) and not applied to this business. The student could have explained the motivation problem leading to workers leaving and the impact this might have on output and sales for ARC. Total = 5/7 marks.

d) Examiner's marks and comments: Full marks – the answer analyses and evaluates clearly.

● Try this

a) 1 mark each for any of these: unemployed workers (chance of a job), shareholders, competitors, residents, government.

b) The answer will depend on which groups are chosen. For example, unemployed workers would now have a chance of getting a job in the new factory, but workers in existing plastics factories might be worried about the new competitor destroying their jobs; the government would welcome the new jobs and increased output (some might be sold abroad as exports); the new factory will pay taxes to the government, but the government might be worried about the negative impact on the environment and the risks of pollution. (Only need to look at one advantage and one disadvantage per stakeholder.) 4 marks for identifying advantages/disadvantages; 4 marks for discussion.

c) Define division of labour (1 mark). Benefits to workers might be: able to specialise and be trained in one task, if output increases this could increase wages. But: work may become repetitive and if plastics factories close (decline of the industry?) then the skills that workers have may no longer be needed. Up to 4 marks for identification of advantages/disadvantages; up to 3 marks for discussion.

UNIT 2 Types of business activity

Sample questions and answers

d) ii) Examiner's marks and comments: The two advantages were both briefly explained. However, there was no attempt to show judgement or evaluation. For example, the student could have referred to the price that Airco might be sold for. Airgroup might pay too much and end up making a loss. Also, Airco workers might go on strike as they do not want to leave the public sector – perhaps because they believe that their jobs are safer under government control. Total = 6/8 marks.

● Try this

a) i) Company X   ii) Company X

b) Less efficient/productive workers; over-staffing; labour-intensive production methods – could be a business that produces hand-made shoes. Any one point explained = up to 4 marks.

c) Managers/owners may wish to remain small to avoid extra work or stress; lack of finance for expansion; the business might sell in quite a small sector of the market with low sales – does not want to expand into other markets it does not know so well. 1 mark for each factor identified (maximum of 2 marks); 1 mark for developing each point.

d) i) Backwards vertical integration (1 mark) because the leather supplier is in the same industry, but supplies raw materials (i.e. at a different stage of production). (2 marks).
ii) More regular and certain supplies of raw material; can control quality of raw material; can obtain cheaper supplies; can prevent supplies being sold to competitors. 1 mark for identification (of each benefit); 1 mark each for some development.

e) i) Secondary (1 mark) – it turns raw materials into finished goods. 1 mark for the explanation.
ii) Tertiary (1 mark) – they provide a service to consumers/manufacturers. 1 mark for the explanation.
iii) This is vertical integration forwards (1 mark). It gives the manufacturer a guaranteed outlet for goods; the manufacturer can control price and marketing of goods etc. 2 marks for identifying points; 2 marks for some development.

f) The public sector is usually made up of important industries such as electricity and public transport. The shoe retailing industry is not as important as this, so it should be in the private sector and private owners will run the shops for profit. 1 mark for definition; up to 4 marks for developing arguments.

UNIT 3 Forms of business organisation

Sample questions and answers

d) Examiner's marks and comments: Although this is quite a short answer, it contains important points and some discussion. There are both advantages and disadvantages and these are briefly looked at from Rashid's point of view. There is a clear recommendation and this is backed up by knowledge of a Deed of Partnership. Total = 8/8 marks.

● **Try this**

a) 1 mark for identifying each reason and 1 mark each for some development. She may have shared some of the work – the business was expanding rapidly. She may have added capital to the business to allow it to buy more equipment which was needed for the expansion.

b) 2 marks for accurate definition – franchising is when a business has permission to use the name, logo and trading methods of an existing business.

c) Up to 3 marks for identifying advantages/disadvantages; 3 marks for discussion of these for O and O Cleaning with a formal judgement. Advantages: rapid way to expand, franchisees use own capital to expand. Disadvantages: less control over the business; franchisee keeps some of the profits of their business. Useful for O and O, as they wanted to expand quickly. They would not have to provide all the finance (it is not a plc), but some control is lost and 'they were keen to control their own business'.

d) 1 mark each for identifying up to three benefits; 1 mark each for developing them. Benefits: less risk; proven successful product; some management tasks done by the franchiser; market research and marketing decisions taken by franchiser.

e) 1 mark for each difference; 1 mark for developing each one.

f) 2 marks for advantages; 2 marks for disadvantages and up to 4 marks for explaining and discussing these for O and O

(1 mark deducted if no recommendation given). For: can raise more capital through sale of shares (they plan to expand); higher public profile and better image; could use share capital to reduce loans. Against: some loss of control; danger of future takeovers; have to release information to public (O and O wanted to control their own business). Give a final recommendation and justify it.

UNIT 4 Government and economic influences on business

Sample questions and answers

d) Examiner's marks and comments: This is an excellent answer. Notice how the student starts off by defining these two terms. The effects of higher interest rates are well applied to Fogla's shop. Finally, there is a very good attempt to evaluate these effects – Fogla's might not be that much affected by higher rates and the student explains why. Total = 8/8 marks.

● **Try this**

a) 2 marks for accurate definition.

b) 2 marks for two examples of government action to protect consumers; up to 2 marks in addition for explaining each point. Governments often protect consumers from dangerous products. If a soft drinks firm did not use very clean methods of production then this could harm consumers. The government would use laws on hygiene standards in this case. Also acceptable: protection against monopoly power, misleading advertisements, underweight or faulty goods.

c) 1 mark for identifying a reason, up to 3 marks for development/explanation. To protect local environment, to avoid building on farmland, to protect residents from pollution, etc. Without these planning restrictions firms would be able to build in the cheapest location without considering any other factors.

d) To create more jobs and to increase demand for the products of local suppliers. 1 mark each.

e) Up to 4 marks for identifying advantages and disadvantages; up to 4 marks for a balanced argument from Mim Chul's point of view. Advantages: improved working conditions, more motivated staff, fewer costly accidents, better public image. Disadvantages: could increase costs, might make Mim Chul's firm uncompetitive compared to rival firms that might have poor health and safety, and lower costs as a result; money could not be used for other things, for example, improved machinery.

UNIT 5 Other external influences on business

● Try this

a) 2 marks for accurate definition.

b) Central Government = Increased exports
Local workers = More choice of jobs
Local authority = Increased local tax payments
Residents = Noise from aircraft
Local unemployed workers = More chance of finding a job
Businesses = Easier to import and export goods
Airlines = Increased flights mean expansion
Train companies = Increased competition from airlines
Environmentalists = Destruction of nature sites
1 mark for each.

c) Up to 2 marks for appropriate letter format. Either (arguments against): Noise, pollution, increased traffic and car parking, spoiling the countryside. Conclusion could be: build it elsewhere or stop the growth in air transport (for example, increase taxes on flying). Or (arguments in favour): Jobs, increased sales for local businesses, more tourists from other countries, easier to import and export products. Conclusion could be: build it as soon as possible, as it will lead to much greater business sales and output. Up to 4 marks for points made; up to 4 marks for analysis and final conclusion.

UNIT 6 Business costs and revenue

● Try this

a) 1 mark each for:
Direct: flour; wages of bakery workers
Indirect: salary, rent

b) 2 marks for defining budgets; 2 marks for brief outline of up to two benefits; 2 marks for applying to Cairo Tyre Company. Budgets are financial plans (for the future).

These plans give departments a target to work towards. This can be motivating for workers. They help to prevent overspending. The marketing department spent too much at the Cairo Tyre Company and this might have been because the department did not know what the budget was.

c) 1 mark for defining diseconomy; 1 mark for any one diseconomy of scale. The example applied to Cairo Tyre Company for 1 further mark.

d) Up to 3 marks for developing benefits; 3 further marks for disadvantages; 2 further marks for balanced discussion. Advantages: useful for analysing how much must be sold to cover all costs (break even) and the safety margin; can be used to compare different options, for example, the break even of different shop locations; able to analyse what might happen to break even if prices are lowered/raised. Disadvantages: assumes all goods are sold; assumes straight lines are realistic; fixed costs are not always constant; can become out of date quickly. On balance: useful if the drawbacks are considered when analysing break-even results.

UNIT 7 Business accounting

Sample questions and answers

c) Examiner's marks and comments: This is very good. The two formulae have been given and the calculations are correct. What is more, the student understands what the results show and tries to suggest one reason for the poor figures. Judgement is shown at the end – it is important to compare ratio results either with other years or with other, similar, businesses. Total = 10/10 marks.

● Try this

a) 1 mark each for: profit and loss account; balance sheet. (Accept also cash flow statement.)

b) Up to 3 marks for *either*: The balance sheet contains details of the firm's assets and liabilities. It also shows the shareholders' funds; *or*: profit and loss account contains the revenue, gross and net profit of the business. The balance sheet also shows the retained profit.

c) Shareholders: i)

Trade union: iii)
Government: iv)
Creditors: ii)
1 mark each.

d) Up to 4 marks for correct ratio results (up to 2 marks if correct formulae but incorrect results); 6 marks for analysing and briefly discussing results. (Accept any four results.)

(Not essential to show formula unless calculation is wrong)	2004	2005
Gross profit margin % = $\dfrac{GP}{\text{Sales revenue}} \times 100$	20%	17.1%
Net profit margin % = $\dfrac{NP}{\text{Sales revenue}} \times 100$	10%	7.1%
Return on capital employed % = $\dfrac{NP}{\text{Capital employed}} \times 100$	15%	10.4%

These results show that the profitability of Titan Tankers has declined since 2004. The company has made less gross and net profit even though sales have increased. Costs seem to have increased too quickly. Also, net profit has fallen despite the fact that more capital has been invested in the business. The new capital does not seem to be very profitable or is not being used very efficiently. But it is important to compare with other companies in the same industry.

UNIT 8 Cash flow planning

● Try this

a) (2,000) This is obtained by subtracting total cash outflow from cash inflow *or*
1,500 − 3,500 = (2,000)

b) Up to 2 marks for definition. This is the cash balance at the end of the month – it could be negative if there is a bank overdraft.

c) Up to 4 marks for using the cash flow forecast to explain answer. There is a bank overdraft at the end of July (a negative closing balance) because cash outflows in the first two months were greater than cash inflows. Although this was not true in July (cash inflow 3,000 and cash outflow 1,500), the negative cash balances in the other months were bigger than the positive net cash flow in July. The main reason seems to be the purchase of equipment.

d) 2 marks for identifying reasons; up to 4 marks for explanation including use of cash flow forecast figures. They can be shown to lenders and investors to encourage them to lend/invest. They can be used to plan future finance needs. In this case Rishav and Abdullah would need to plan an overdraft, at least for the first three months. If they did not plan this, the bank could refuse it just when they needed it. In this case it shows that the net cash flow is positive in July and this might encourage lenders and investors to believe that the radio station will be successful.

UNIT 9 Financing business activity

Sample questions and answers

3) ii) Examiner's marks and comments: 2 marks for knowledge and application; 1 mark for some attempt to analyse why it would be useful. The student could have explained that forecast profit and cash flow would be very important to the loan decision. Also, there is no evaluation. The business plan might not be detailed enough or the bank manager might think that it was too optimistic, so the loan might not be given after all. Total = 3/6 marks.

● Try this

a) 1 mark for each advantage and disadvantage.
Shares: Can raise substantial sums of capital for limited companies *but* may affect the ownership and control of the business.
Overdraft: Flexible form of finance that can be varied to meet the needs of the business *but* often high interest rate and can be called back by the bank at short notice.
Long-term loan: Suitable for long-term projects or expansion and does not affect ownership or control *but* interest must be paid and the loan will have to be repaid.

b) 1 mark for each correct answer:
Debenture: external
Shares: external
Profit: internal
Sale of buildings: internal

c) Up to 2 marks for stating suitable sources, up to 4 marks for explaining any two of these for this business; 2 marks for reasoning and recommendation.

Long-term loans (short-term or medium-term may be unsuitable), sale of shares, retained profits. An overdraft is not suitable for long-term expansion.

Explain one benefit and one drawback to at least *two* of these.

Recommendation. Might depend on current interest rate – if high, then shares or profits might be better. If profits are low then they might be inadequate for the expansion. If directors do not want to risk losing control, then sale of shares could be risky. Advice: retained profits if sufficient, if not, then loan if the interest rate not too high.

UNIT 10 Organisational structure

Sample questions and answers

d) Examiner's marks and comments: Two factors are identified, explained and given some link to Yuan's flower business. Finally, the student tries to explain that the final structure is not certain – it depends on how Yuan expands the business. All four skills are shown by the student. Total = 8/8 marks.

● **Try this**

a) 4 marks for correct and labelled chart; 2–3 marks for missing some information or one level; 1 mark for some attempt.

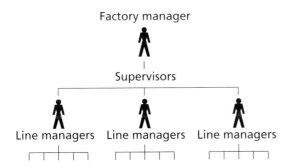

b) i) 1 mark for identifying problem; 1 mark for application to Abadullah's business; 2 marks for explanation/analysis.
Poor communication with lower levels – managers of factories will not be able to communicate easily with Head Office; decisions not taken locally or taken by more junior managers. The styles of clothes chosen by Abadullah might not be right for all regions; possible poor motivation for factory managers as all major decisions are taken at Head Office.

ii) 1 mark for definition; 1 mark for application to this business; 2 marks for explanation/analysis.
Yes, it does appear to be centralised as all major decisions are taken at Head Office which is a sign of a centralised business. Factory managers cannot decide which styles to make or how to pay their production workers.

iii) 1 mark for definition; up to 3 marks for identifying advantages/drawbacks of decentralisation; 2 marks for explaining/analysing at least two of these and 2 marks for discussion/judgement.
Decentralisation is when decision-making power is given to factories, branches or divisions, and not Head Office. Possible benefits: Quicker decision-making locally, decisions taken locally will take local factors such as fashion or labour shortages into account. Drawbacks: managers will need training to take good decisions; different branches and areas may take different decisions and these could clash. Decentralising could benefit Abadullah's business if managers are trained well and if local differences are so great that Head Office decisions do not suit all areas.

UNIT 11 Managing a business

● **Try this**

a) 1 mark for reason; up to 3 marks for explaining it.
Any one of: motivating staff; giving the business a sense of purpose and direction; making sure all departments are working towards the same aims; giving managers a means of comparing actual performance against the original target.
Any one of these should be briefly explained, analysing why this advantage results from aims and targets.

b) 1 mark each (see Key definitions).

c) Up to 3 marks for identifying important factors; up to 3 marks for applying them to this business; up to 4 marks for analysing them with a final, supported recommendation. Person A is very ambitious and if Umeel wants the restaurant to expand, this might be the person to employ. 'A' seems to be a good communicator – very important in a busy restaurant. 'A' is well educated and possibly trained in management and motivation techniques – the 25 restaurant staff will need to be well managed. 'B' has more relevant experience and being a former chef means 'B' might concentrate on quality meals and motivate the staff to achieve this target. Quality is 'B''s objective and this might mean that Umeel could increase prices in the restaurant. If Umeel wants the business to expand over the next few years, I would choose 'A' as long as there are already good chefs who can take control of the cooking side of the business.

UNIT 12 Communication in business
● Try this
a) 1 mark for correct answer plus 1 mark for brief explanation.
External – the manager is sending a message to people who do not work in the business.
b) Up to 4 marks for up to two advantages and two disadvantages of any two methods; up to 4 marks for discussion in context and final recommendation.
An e-mail would be quick, but it may not be opened immediately. An attachment could be included, in colour, of the product details. A telephone call would be more personal and the benefits of the new sweet could be explained to every shop owner; however, it would take a long time to telephone all shop owners. The best method could be a video sent to all shops plus posters for displaying in the shop. It could be expensive and take a long time to produce the video though, and the manufacturer could never be sure that every shop owner watched it.
c) 1 mark each for identifying possible barriers to communication; up to 2 marks for each barrier for explaining them and applying them to either example. Notice board: cannot be certain that it will be read by everyone that is meant to receive the message as there is usually no chance for feedback. It is a written format which not everyone will be attracted by, and some may not understand the language used. Both of these problems could result in poor communication. The same barriers can apply to newsletters.

UNIT 13 Motivation at work
Sample questions and answers
3) i) Examiner's marks and comments: 1 mark for identifying $200 paid, then 1 mark for stating piece rate. The third mark would be for explaining why it was clear it was piece rate. Total = 2/3 marks.
ii) 2 marks for correct answer.

● Try this
a) 6 marks for explaining the advantages and disadvantages of different financial and non-financial methods of motivation; 4 marks for selecting one method and explaining why you think it the best one to use; 2 marks if the answer is in the context of Patel Fashions. Financial methods might include commission, profit-sharing bonus or performance-related pay. Non-financial methods might include discounts on the clothes, paying for healthcare, pension, clothes.
b) 4 marks for explaining how to use job rotation/job enlargement/job enrichment to increase motivation (1–2 marks each); 2 marks for saying whether you consider job rotation to be the best method to use and why; 2 marks for answering in the context of Patel Fashions. Job rotation involves workers swapping round and doing each task for only a limited time and then changing round again. Job enlargement is where extra tasks of a similar level of skill are added to a worker's job description. Job rotation is quite limited in the shop as there are not very many jobs to do. Job enlargement might be better as workers will then get more enjoyment from doing a variety of jobs such as working on the tills, arranging the clothes and helping customers, which will increase their job satisfaction.
c) i) 1 mark for autocratic. 2 marks for justifying the choice of management style. Workers need to be constantly supervised so they will work.
ii) 1 mark for democratic or laissez-faire. 2 marks for justifying the choice of management style. Workers are motivated by being able to take an interest in their work.

UNIT 14 Recruitment, training and human resources

Sample questions and answers

2) ii) Examiner's marks and comments: The student's answer gives two suggestions which are explained. Total = 4/6 marks.

● Try this

a) 1 mark for each reason given, for example, redundancy, sacked, employee left because they found another job/moved away from the area/emigrated.

b) 1 mark for stating a problem (maximum 2 marks) and up to 2 additional marks if the reason is explained as to why it is a problem. Possible problems might include: the reasons why the employees are leaving, for example, bad management; costs of replacing the employees; increased training costs; reduced morale.

c) 2 marks for describing what induction training includes: for example, show the employee where everything is; health and safety training; meet other employees; go over rules and regulations of the business. 2 marks for explaining the usefulness to the business of induction training.

d) i) 6 marks for discussing the advantages and/or disadvantages of internal and external recruitment, for example, cost, skills of applicants, motivation, availability of suitable employees; 2 marks if applied to chefs; 4 marks for justifying which would be the better method to use and why. The conclusion would probably be external recruitment so the chefs would already be trained and able to bring their experience to the restaurants. The chefs would be productive straight away and would not need to be trained by The Royal Garden, which would be expensive.

ii) 2 marks for explaining either on-the-job or off-the-job training; 3 marks for justifying which would be the more suitable method to use and why. The answer would probably be on-the-job training, but if suitable justification is given then full marks could be awarded for off-the-job training. Advantages of on-the-job training: because it would be easy and cheap to let other workers show the new employees what to do; these employees do not need much training as the jobs are low-skilled.

Unit 15 Employee and employer associations

Sample questions and answers

2) ii) Examiner's marks and comments: A good answer in context of the business and the candidate explains how it will help to avoid conflict. Total = 5/5 marks.

● Try this

a) craft union – (iv); industrial union – (ii); general union – (iii); white collar union – (i) 1 mark for each correct answer.

b) 1 mark for each of three benefits (for example, represent employees in negotiations with trade unions; give advice to members; act as pressure group for members; share ideas) and 3 additional marks for explanations.

c) i) 2 marks for explaining the advantages and disadvantages of strike action (for example, very disruptive to business; loss of pay for workers); 2 marks for explaining the advantages and disadvantages of an overtime ban (for example, workers don't lose normal pay; pressure on business as orders may be delivered late); 2 marks for deciding which would be more effective for the workers at P and D Ltd and why. An overtime ban would probably be more effective because P and D Ltd have got increasing sales and they need to increase output to meet these orders. The workers will not lose any wages, but there will be pressure on the company to give in to the employees' wishes otherwise they will lose business. Strike action could also be effective as output would be lost, but the workers would not get paid when on strike so an overtime ban would be the best form of industrial action for the workers to take.

ii) 1 mark for each of three examples of worker participation (for example, worker directors, works councils, quality circles, more democratic styles of leadership); 3 additional marks for explaining the three ways of having worker participation.

UNIT 16 The market and marketing

● Try this

a) 1 mark for stating each objective of marketing (for example, to increase sales revenue and profitability; to increase market share; to improve the image of products; to target a new market or market segment; to develop new products or improve existing products); 3 additional marks for explaining the three objectives.

b) 1 mark for each element – Product, Price, Promotion, Place.

c) 4 marks for explaining the benefits of linking the elements of the marketing mix together (for example, so that the different elements reinforce each other; the advertising budget will be more effectively used; sales will be higher); 4 marks for explaining what might happen if the business does not link the elements together (for example, the sales may not be as high as they could be; potential customers may buy the competitors' products; the product might fail altogether).

UNIT 17 Market research
Sample questions and answers

b) Examiner's marks and comments: The candidate only states what is meant by primary and secondary research and does not explain the difference between them. Total = 2/4 marks.

● Try this

a) 2 marks for each advantage stated (for example, first-hand information straight from actual or potential consumers; can be qualitative rather than quantitative; information about the product itself is obtained); 2 marks for explaining each advantage.

b) 1 mark for each example (government statistics on population and income; newspapers of the country; trade magazines in the other country; the report and accounts of the competitors in the other country; information provided by an international organisation, such as the UN, on its website).

c) 2 marks for each way the business can try to ensure the information is accurate. Up to 2 marks for explaining each of these ways (for example, make sure the information is up to date, take a large sample, ensure the sample is representative of the target market).

UNIT 18 Presentation of information
● Try this

a) 1 mark for a title; 2 marks for correctly labelled axes and scale; 2 marks for correctly plotted graph.

b) **i)** 2 marks for describing the trend in each graph. Product A has seen sales increase slowly at first and then rise rapidly. After reaching a peak, sales then fall. Product B sees sales increase steadily, reach a peak and then fall. But sales then start to rise again and continue to rise above the previous peak.

ii) 1 mark for stating a reason for the differences; 2 marks for explaining the reason (for example, Product A has a typical product life cycle; Product B had successful extension strategies used, so that sales have increased again after the decline stage).

UNIT 19 The marketing mix: product and packaging
Sample questions and answers

d) Examiner's marks and comments: The candidate suggests several ways of increasing sales and explains how they should be effective, and there is also a consideration of drawbacks. The answer is applied to this business but no decision is made as to what is the best way of increasing sales. Total = 6/8 marks.

● Try this

a) 3 marks for explaining the functions of packaging; 2 marks for applying the answer to sports drinks (for example, to give information about what the drink contains; to make the drink look attractive; to give the drink a sporty image; to preserve the drink).

b) 3 marks for stating the factors Sheena might take into account. 3 marks for explaining why these factors might be important (for example, cost of packaging, competitors' packaging, the target market for the drink, design allowing consumers to drink out of the container).

c) 1 mark for labelling the axes, 3 marks for labelling the five stages, deduct 1 mark for each missing label. Stages to label – introduction, growth, maturity, saturation, decline.

d) 3 marks for describing the changes; 3 marks for saying what should happen as a result of the changes (for example, the price may be high when the product is first introduced to the market if there are few or no competitors. Then competitive pricing as competition increases in the growth phase. When sales start to fall, the price may be reduced to try to encourage sales to increase again or at least slow the decline in sales).

e) 3 marks for explaining why some products have longer life cycles (for example, they are not fashion goods and therefore stay popular for longer; they appeal to a large market and have few competitors – customers will keep buying the products as there will be no close substitutes). 1 mark for a suitable example (for example, chocolate bars, washing powder).

UNIT 20 The marketing mix: price

Sample questions and answers

c) Examiner's marks and comments: 2 marks for correctly identifying that demand is inelastic; 2 marks for making a judgement as to what the business should have done and why. The student does not explain the effects of the change on the business. The student could have explained that Luxury Leisure plc lost members due to the price increase. However, the reduction in members was a lower percentage than the percentage increase in price. Total = 4/6 marks.

● Try this

a) 2 marks for stating whether demand is inelastic (then a percentage increase in price would lead to a smaller percentage fall in sales and an increase in sales revenue) or elastic (then a larger percentage fall in sales and a fall in sales revenue). 2 marks for explaining why petrol would be likely to have an inelastic demand, which means that customers are not price sensitive and most of them will keep buying the product (if prices rise, sales revenue will increase). Elastic demand means that customers are price sensitive and they will buy substitute products.

b) 2 marks for stating that they want to increase sales of the products; 2 marks for explaining that this will be at times of the year when sales will not be good, for example, at the end of a season for gift items associated with particular festivals.

c) 4 marks for stating factors that affect pricing strategies. 4 marks for explaining these factors and why they are important to the business (for example, competitors' prices; stage of the product life cycle of the product; costs of production; type of product; quality of product; whether there are competing products).

UNIT 21 The marketing mix: promotion

Sample questions and answers

b) Examiner's marks and comments: Three suitable ways suggested and two were justified briefly. Total = 5/9 marks.

● Try this

a) 1 mark for teenagers.

b) Up to 3 marks for stating factors like the cost; trends in spending habits; which is most likely to increase profits; what type of customers use the shopping centre. Up to 4 marks for explaining how these factors influence the decision. If many different age groups of customers use the shopping centre then sales may be increased by attracting a wider range of customers. If Music Mania spends more on advertising then it will only attract the same age group of customers and this may not increase sales as much.

c) 3 marks for stating the factors to consider. 3 marks for explaining these factors. 2 marks for applying them to selling classical music. The promotion has to be suitable for music. If the profit per CD was not high then 'buy one, get one free' would not be suitable as the business would lose money. CDs are not bought that often, so it might be better to offer a second CD at a reduced price once one has been purchased.

d) 1 mark for a suitable example (for example, fitted kitchen, building work); 3 marks for explaining why the example would be sold using personal selling – advice would need to be given and the product or service may be specific to the customers' requirements.

UNIT 22 The marketing mix: place

Sample questions and answers

2) ii) Examiner's marks and comments: A good answer, but more than two factors were considered and the answer had more points explained than were needed to achieve full marks. Total 8/8 marks.

● Try this

a) i) wedding cakes; ii) new cars; iii) tins of fruit; iv) shoes (exported)

b) 5 marks for explaining the advantages and disadvantages of not selling to a retail chain of supermarkets (for example, sales are not as high, does not reach a wide target market, more control over the way the product is sold to the customer). 5 marks for explaining the advantages and disadvantages of selling directly to an airline (sold directly to customer so higher profits, products are produced to the customer's specification).

c) Product – should be high quality furniture; Price – should be high to reflect a high quality product; Promotion – should be in places where high-income groups would be likely to see the advertisements; Place – should be in shops which sell mainly expensive products. 4 marks for stating the different elements of the marketing mix. 4 marks for explaining how these four elements would be used in each case. 4 marks for the answer to be in the context of furniture for each element of the marketing mix.

d) 4 marks for stating different factors to consider. 4 marks for explaining why these factors would be important when deciding on the marketing mix in a different country. The types of retail outlets used, for example, may be different. In one country large supermarkets may be used by most of the customers whereas in another country, small shops may be more common, so wholesalers will be part of the 'place' in the marketing mix in one country, but not in the other.

UNIT 23 Factors affecting production

Sample questions and answers

c) i) Examiner's marks and comments: Clear definition. Total = 2/2 marks.

● Try this

a) i) 1 mark for each method – job production and flow production.

ii) 2 marks for explaining what is meant by either quality control or quality assurance; 2 marks for saying why it is important to Medic Supplies plc. Quality assurance is where quality standards are set and then applied throughout the business. Everyone on the production line at Medic Supplies plc will be responsible for ensuring that there are no defects with the products. This is particularly important for this business because it supplies equipment to hospitals and if there were any faults then a death could be caused, meaning the company would get a bad reputation resulting in lost sales.

iii) 2 marks for explaining the process of stock control; 2 marks for explaining how it ensures that raw materials should always be available so that production can take place; 2 marks for being in the context of medical supplies.

iv) 2 marks for definition of lean production. Up to 4 marks for explaining how it might be introduced at the business.

b) i) 3 marks for stating the cost savings of using computers to take orders instead of employing people (for example, fewer people needed, less wages to pay out, ordering can be automated); 3 marks for explaining why these mean lower costs.

ii) 2 marks for stating the possible effects on the number and types of jobs at the company, 2 marks for explaining why these effects are worrying for the employees at Telesales Services Ltd. More on-line ordering will mean that fewer employees will be needed as this is done automatically. Fewer telephone orders will mean employees who work in this section will be made redundant as they will not be transferred to on-line ordering. This is why employees are worried about losing their jobs.

UNIT 24 Factors affecting location

Sample questions and answers

3) Examiner's marks and comments: 3 marks for listing disadvantages (more than three were listed) and 1 mark for explaining the reason for high rent in city centres. The candidate needed to explain the other disadvantages for full marks. Total = 4/6 marks.

● Try this

a) i) 3 marks for each of the three factors (for example, availability of labour, location of ports, availability and cost of land, government grants); 3 marks for explaining why these factors are important. The cocoa is imported so being located near to a port will reduce the transport costs of the raw materials.

ii) 1 mark for stating each of the appropriate factors (maximum 3); for example, the

market, costs of setting up a new factory, costs of running a factory in this overseas market, availability of suitable labour, government policy; 3 marks for explaining these factors; 2 marks for applying the answer to chocolate manufacturing; 2 marks for making judgements as to which factors are the most important when making the decision. If particular skilled labour is needed and there is none available in the country then it will be expensive to employ foreign skilled workers.

b) 2 marks for stating the disadvantages of businesses locating wherever they want to, without any consideration of the local population or environment; 4 marks for explaining the reasons. For example, causing traffic congestion from delivery lorries; destroying areas with wildlife and natural beauty; the local population may not be happy about factories being built near their houses; causing pollution.

c) 2 marks for stating whether location is important to this business; 4 marks for justifying this answer. Points may include: selling over the internet means that customers do not need to go to a particular place to see the products so the business does not need a shop for customers to visit; orders are sent by post and therefore it is useful to have access to postal services nearby; the internet allows the business to locate anywhere in the world, not necessarily in the same country as the customers; orders can be placed over the internet, so the business is not reliant on the post for orders to be sent, which saves time between orders being placed and the orders being received by the business.

UNIT 25 Business in the international community
Key definitions
The 'examples' questions are based on your own country – ask your teacher to check your answers.

Sample questions and answers
d) ii) Examiner's marks and comments: The student has understood the impact on exporters of an appreciation and has stated that this could reduce profits from exporting. Total = 4/4 marks.

● Try this
a) 1 mark for indentifying each reason and 1 mark for a brief explanation of each one. To obtain raw materials – these might not be available in the 'home' country; to produce more cheaply – labour costs could be lower in another country; to avoid tariffs – by producing goods in another country, import tariffs will no longer have to be paid for imports into that country.

b) 1 mark for each correct point. Language problems; different laws (for example, consumer protection); different customer tastes; communication problems with head office.

c) Up to 2 marks for benefits and up to 2 marks for drawbacks; up to 4 marks for discussion and judgement. Benefits: more jobs, export earnings, increased output, increased tax revenues. Drawbacks: jobs lost at existing competitors, possible environmental damage; possible exploitation of labour; possible excessive exploitation of natural resources; profits sent back to 'home' country.

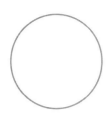

Index